Originally this book was ... law. As a religious scepti... world religions: Buddhis... Judaism. He attempts to see what can be known, if anything, about a "God" or an "afterlife" from logic and tangible evidence, from a layman's perspective rather than a formal philosophical approach. He shares his findings with his sister-in-law and tries to address her objections."

Bill Medley worked as a professional entertainer for fifteen years. His stand-up comedy routines sometimes included satires on religion. Here he gives it a more serious examination.

"Absolutely brilliant!... If all those who argue over religion had a copy of this book it would revolutionise the relationship between me and my bank manager." Bill Medley

"This book has dramatically changed my whole attitude towards typing." Diana Medley (wife)

Religion is for Fools!

Bill Medley

MONARCH
BOOKS

Oxford, UK & Grand Rapids, Michigan, USA

First published by VIVA Press in Australia in 1996 (medley@netspace.net.au).

First published in the UK by Monarch Books
(a publishing imprint of Lion Hudson plc),
Mayfield House, 256 Banbury Road, Oxford OX2 7DH
Tel: +44 (0) 1865 302750 Fax: +44 (0) 1865 302757
Email: monarch@lionhudson.com
www.lionhudson.com

UK ISBN 1 85424 681 X
US ISBN 0 8254 6077 8

Distributed by:
UK: Marston Book Services Ltd, P.O. Box 269, Abingdon, Oxon OX14 4YN;
USA: Kregel Publications, P.O. Box 2607, Grand Rapids, Michigan 49501.

Unless otherwise stated, all Scripture quotations are from the Holy Bible,
New International Version, © 1973, 1978, 1984 by the
International Bible Society. Used by permission of
Hodder and Stoughton Ltd. All rights reserved.
Buddhist Scriptures, translated by Edward Conze, copyright © 1959.
Holy Koran, translated by N.J. Dawood,
copyright © 1956, 1959, 1966, 1968, 1974, 1990.
Sacred Texts of the East, ed. F.M. Muller © Delhi: Motital Publishers 1992.

Cover illustration by Darren Harvey Regan
Interior illustrations by Robert Kabbas

British Library Cataloguing Data
A catalogue record for this book is available from the British Library.

Printed and bound in Great Britain by Bookmarque Ltd

Contents

1

Dear Rita

Dear Rita,

I want to share with you some heartfelt thoughts concerning our recent discussions, so please try to stay with me.

It's so hard to talk about a subject like religion, even with those you love, without the discussion becoming emotional. Instead, I'm going to put down all my thoughts on paper, describe my own investigation of religion and try to address the many points and questions you've raised. I hope this will allow you a chance to look it over critically in your own time. This way there's no fear of an argument breaking out, because it's hard to talk back to a piece of paper. Well there's no point in half doing this, so get ready for the world's longest letter.

I don't want you to misunderstand my motivation for writing this, Rita. Think of it this way. Imagine that you came to conclusions on something that concerns people's lives. What is the first thing you would do? More to the point, who are the first people you would want to share it with? Surely the people you care the most about! And why them? So that you can convert them to your way of thinking? Or so you can convince them that you know more than they do, and show them you're right and they're wrong? Believe me, Rita, when it concerns the lives of those you love, the last thing on your mind is converting people to *your* way of thinking, or showing them that *you* are right.

My motivation is not – "if she only believed what I do, she would feel so much better about herself". As far as I know, Rita, you already feel fine now. For that matter, so did I before my investigation. I was not looking to "feel better".

The important thing here is not whether religious views make us feel good, but whether they are true. This is the real issue I want to discuss. Obviously you are happy and unconcerned in your own life at this point, so I'm appealing to you to have patience with me in what follows, even if you think it unnecessary.

The crutch of the matter

A couple of years ago, Rita, I found difficulty with some of the same questions that you have trouble with now. Up until that time, you had far more religious experience than I did, having had the advantage of a religious schooling and upbringing. When I decided to investigate religion, I did not have any set beliefs or any real religious knowledge. Perhaps my ignorance had its own kind of advantage: I felt nothing strongly about religion at all. I was quite ready to reject religious answers altogether.

If I had any prejudice at all before I started, it was a certain aversion to organized religions. I think this made me more cautious and critical. I know how easy it is to allow prejudice to hinder an open-minded look at religion. It's easy, for instance, to dismiss religion as something making people narrow and cruel. Tremendous harm has been done in the name of religion. But then

8

more people have been murdered in the last century by those who loved to hate religion. Stalin, consistent with most Communist programmes, was fiercely atheistic, and Hitler, with his hatred for religious authority, killed upwards of 30 million people, and we can add Pol Pot and Mao Tse Tung's millions to these.

So what do I say to this? "Oooh, all those horrible atheists. That does it! I'm turning my back on atheism and going off to join a religion!"

The way I see it, it would be as foolish to use Stalin and Mao as "evidence" against atheism as it would be to conclude anything against religion because of abuses in religion. Any good thing in life can be abused. In fact the better things are, the more they seem to be abused. Should we regard sex as bad because sexual abuse is so widespread?

I used to dismiss religious belief very easily. I knew that in all societies man shows a desire to worship some greater being and my response was, "Of course, people just want to believe in something, as a crutch!" I saw religious belief basically as wishful thinking. However, someone with a prejudice *towards* religion can just as easily see it all in a different way. Try this.

Man has an in-built desire for:
Food   –   There is food
Sex   –   There is sex
Worship –   There is a God

So if it suits our prejudice we can go either way. We can explain away beliefs as a crutch, or we can rationalize that beliefs must relate to something real. But in the end nothing is proved.

God is not going to exist simply because people believe there is a God, or think they have a need to believe in something. Neither will God cease to exist just because you or I think there is *no* need or reason to believe in a God.

Rita, let's get away from prejudging – from deciding beforehand what we want or don't want to believe, and try and get to the facts.

Religion is for fools

Some people have told me that their feelings are a good guide to the "unknowable" questions concerning God. "Spirituality is something that you must feel, and if you have a strong feeling, then it must be true." But even for those people whose feelings are usually a good guide, the question still has to be asked: "Have you ever had a feeling that turned out to be wrong?" I remember the first time I fell in love at high school. I had this overwhelming feeling (in fact I was *certain*) that this girl was going to feel the same way that I did. It was a definite! Now you are not going to believe this – but it turned out I was wrong! What could that girl possibly have been thinking!

Well, we've all been wrong sometime – even when we've been "certain". So even if you have that great intuition and are 99% reliable, you still could never be certain of anything based on feelings. What about a spiritual experience? Some say they know God, or know about God, because they have had a great spiritual experience. But even that doesn't prove anything. Most people believe there is good and bad in all of us. If there is good and bad in us, then this could apply to the spiritual realm. If you had a genuine spiritual experience, then how do you know it is from a good or truthful source? "Oh I know it's good because it felt so right, and the experience gave me the assurance that it was good and from God." But how do you know it was not a bad source *telling* you it was good? You can't be certain – even with the most profound spiritual experience.

So what about our intellect? I remember doing a gig one night at a conference with about 1,000 doctors. I got talking with a specialist MD who told me that you could be certain about God. He said you could be certain that there was no God, because God is an absolute, and there is no such thing as an absolute. I said to him, "Are you *absolutely* sure about that?" – He gazed into the night... In other words, you would have to know absolutely everything before you could really know the answers to these great questions.

Suffice it to say that the only thing we know for sure is that we just don't know everything. Whether it is our feelings, our spiritual experiences or our intellect, the bottom line is that from ourselves, there is no way any of us could ever know anything for certain about God or the afterlife, or any of these great mysteries. This is what led me to believe that *religion is for fools*. People are just grasping at ideas and placing all their hopes in them, without having any real basis. And no matter how heartfelt these beliefs are – in the end they are just (albeit sincerely) – guessing.

And I suppose we have to include people who are sure that no religion is true. They are guessing as well. Then there are the people who say that all the religions are true. They must be the biggest "guessers" of all. They are just "hedging" their guesses. And then there are those who say that truth in religion is relative. That is, "all beliefs are true – as long as it's true for you." Great! And where did you get that "truth" from? "Well, er... I guess it's my own idea..." Wonderful! You might do well at politics, but in the end it's just another stab in the dark. Another guess. All because it "feels" right.

So we are all in this together, Rita. It's not enough to say that each person's opinion is as good as another. Take a look at what we are dealing with here. We might as well be trying to guess how many specks of dust are on the moon. Let's say it straight. Each person's opinion is as *bad* as another's!

The only way we could ever know anything for certain about any of these great "unknowable" questions concerning God, is if someone who knew *absolutely everything* was to tell us. It would have to be someone completely outside our limited knowledge. Someone who was not dependent on our finite feelings or our unreliable experiences. In fact, it would have to be no one less than God – "him", "her", "itself" (whoever or whatever God is), to be the one to reveal who or what God is, and answer for us those "unknowable" afterlife questions.

Religious pi and sources

Rita, you know me well enough to know I don't do anything by half measures and I love to investigate things thoroughly. There have been thousands of religions throughout history, but I discovered there are actually only five major sources of religion, out of which come nearly all of the world's religions. Ever since I was a young man I thought it would be kind of cool one day to be able to say that I had investigated them for myself. Not that I wanted to "join up", I just wanted to say that I'd been there and done that, when those people come knocking on my door. It took me about fifteen more years before I actually got started on that investigation, because I got a little busy trying to become rich and famous. But I also remember somewhat cynically thinking, "If there was some message from God in any of these religions that was intended for 'wide distribution', then even someone like me should able to get that message just by reading their sources for myself." I at least cautiously acknowledged this much. *If* there is a greater being or God, and *if* this greater being has communicated directly to mankind, it could be through one or more (or even all) of these five major sources. That is not to say that if there is a God, that God has bothered to formally communicate to mankind at all. And even if God did, for me the question remains: what could possibly show up in these sources that could prove itself to be clearly *outside* human limitations? How could any of these "messages" possibly be distinguished from just a lot of sincere "guessing"? So all I am saying at this point is, *if* there is a God who has communicated in that way, then we could look at the five major religions: Buddhism, Christianity, Hinduism, Islam and Judaism.

All these religions have "holy books" that they claim are inspired by God or contain all spiritual knowledge. These books are the major foundations of nearly all of the world's religions. I realized that I couldn't be content with my preconceived Western notions of these religions. If I was to test the claims of these religious writings as being a revelation from a so-called "higher power", I would need to read the actual sources myself. I didn't want to speak to any priests or Buddhist monks or Hindu gurus, etc., in case I got a particular slant or interpretation from someone who might belong to their religion for personal reasons, or merely because of tradition. So eventually I set out to read from start to finish:

- *Buddhist scriptures:* Depending on whether it's Pali or Tibetan Buddhist scriptures, there are 45 and 325 large volumes respectively, of about 1,000 pages each. (My only concern here was that if the secrets to the afterlife were in here, then what if I died before I could finish reading them? Fortunately, Buddhist scholars have translated what are considered the important sections, so I didn't have to read all of them.)
- *The Hindu Veda: Bhagavad Gita*, *Upanishads* and *Rig Veda.*
- *The Jewish scriptures: Hebrew Holy Scriptures* or the Old Testament. (Since the Mishnah and Talmud are commentary on the Old Testament laws as well as detailed instruction on daily living, marriage, agriculture, etc., I decided to start with only the prophetic writings of the Hebrew scriptures.)
- *The Koran:* Islam, the teachings of Mohammed.
- *The New Testament:* the teachings of Jesus.

When I first decided to investigate religion, my goal was to leave aside any preferences or expectations of my own as to what a God or higher being should be like.

For instance, the Muslim God in the Koran says:

...make war on the unbelievers...[1]

and about those who oppose Islam:

...put them to death wherever you find them.[2]

Now this may not appeal to my personal view of what a divine being should say, but the question for me was, did "God" really say this or not? If he really did, then too bad for my personal view (and for unbelievers for that matter: just ask Salman Rushdie).

Blinded by the loot

When I began reading these holy books, I soon saw that many of their teachings have been misquoted or taken out of context by those who have used religion as a means of gaining money and power. Many people have been misled in this way over the years but I am now convinced this often occurs because people do not read the actual texts themselves. If they did, they would find them generally straightforward to understand.

It's possible to have too much sympathy for those who are misled. Signing a contract without reading it is foolishness. Surely, giving your life to someone or some religion without checking it out at its source is also an individual responsibility.

As I thought about this, Rita, I had to admit that for many years I myself had been critical of organized religions without having properly investigated them. Not too long ago I belonged to a religion of "unbelief". I suppose one way or another we are all betting our lives on some belief system, even if it's just the religion of "sitting on the fence". To reject the "believer's" position without checking it out properly is just as ignorant as being the dupe of some religious cult. And so my own investigation eventually got underway.

2

Arnold Schwarzenegger has "no problemo"

Rita, don't fall for what's been dubbed the religious "I know, I know, I know syndrome". This is *not* a criticism of your Catholic upbringing because it's just as pertinent to people brought up in other religious denominations. It *is*, however, a criticism of those with a "religious upbringing", who in their whole adult life have never read any religious source documents (not even the New Testament), and yet they assume they already "know all about it".

All I ask is that you keep an open mind to the possibility that traditional Western notions don't necessarily qualify you to say that you "know all about" *any* religion.

Agnostic – *a type of walking stick for those who are "not sure" if they need a religious crutch*

Depending on the survey, statistics show that between 75% and 96% of people believe in some concept of God or a greater being.[3] From what I gather, Rita, you're one of those people. Just the same, let's not limit ourselves for the moment to any particular concept of this "greater force" or "God", unless facts emerge that allow us to make a more specific definition.

Unlike the person who is not open to the possibility of a greater being, I think you agree more with acclaimed artist, the late Brett Whiteley. As far as I know, Whiteley had no particular religious affiliation, but in an interview just before his death he said:

> There's no other explanation for the occurrences and source and the mystery of existence, except that there is some force eminently larger and more intelligent than I can ever imagine.[4]

Nothing grows out of thin hair

You may already be familiar with the basic axiom of scientific and philosophical reasoning, the Latin phrase *ex nihilo, nihil fit*, or "out of nothing, nothing comes".

Commenting on this, Professor R.C. Sproul observes that if there were ever a time when there was nothing, then there would be nothing here now. If there is something here now, then there must have been something or someone here in the beginning. Someone who has *always* been there, outside of time. One who has the power of being within.[5]

I suppose what Sproul is getting at is that even if you believe in a big bang, someone must have lit the fuse. Or if we believe the theory about the world coming from hydrogen, where did the hydrogen come from? It can't have popped out of nothing.

These are interesting points to think about, but if, contrary to what I've thought, you feel you are a true atheist, don't feel as though I've lost you already. I want to make it perfectly clear that if you are an atheist, it won't change or take away from my investigation one bit.

Well let's get back to where we left off.

Firstly, I want to take us from point A to point B in logical progression using tangible evidence that can easily be verified from institutions such as our National Library. Let me explain my approach by using an analogy. If you look at the illustration…

Figure A   Figure B

Figure A is Arnold Schwarzenegger before bodybuilding
Figure B is Arnold after bodybuilding.

Bodybuilding works
(unless your "use by" date has expired)

I propose that the evidence is undeniable that bodybuilding works. There are photos of Arnold before and after. The problem is, there is disagreement among some scientists as to how muscles actually grow.

Sure, you lift weights, but what actually occurs inside the muscle cells, and what role does lactic acid really play? These questions have been disputed. No matter how confident a majority of scientists may be, others have disagreed on how the process works.

My point is this. Scientists may never all agree and find conclusive proof of all the crucial details, and yet dumb old you and me *don't* need scientists to tell us bodybuilding works! (At least for Arnold it does.) We can be certain.

The evidence is tangible and indisputable, despite the fact that we don't know everything about how or why it all happens. Scientists keep arguing details, but Arnold has "No Problemo".

I propose that on this investigation we stick with what the evidence tells us. Whether we can fill in all the gaps of the whys and hows is irrelevant. If we can get from A to B as a fact, then all the questions and disagreements in the world that fall in between those points will not change the fact.

3

To "B" or not to "B"

Before I started investigating, I was at point A with this question:

IF THERE IS A GOD, HAS THIS GOD COMMUNICATED TO MAN?

As we consider the sacred texts I am not asking you to assume that any of them are necessarily a communication from God (if there is a God). For now, just let me give you some brief comments on what I eventually got through reading.

Buddha

We can't know all the specific teachings of the original Buddha (Buddha is a title, meaning "the enlightened one"). His personal name was Siddhartha Gautama. Siddhartha lived between the 4th and 6th centuries BC, and other important Buddhist leaders have added to the Buddhist scriptures through the centuries. They made for some interesting reading. Most of the scriptures were compiled between the 2nd century BC and the 2nd century AD. The scriptures gave me the impression that Buddha was a man of great thought. It seemed to me that he was able to clarify his teachings and thoughts on life much more than his Hindu contemporaries, whom he had rejected as false.

The Veda (Hindu scriptures) have no known authors and often seemed to be deliberately mythological, perhaps meant to be understood symbolically. At least that's what Buddha and I thought, anyway.

While I learned a lot from all of this reading, it didn't really shed much light on the question of whether there was a God, or whether such a being might have communicated to man.

After all, the fact that I think Buddha was a man of great intellect doesn't prove anything. The Buddha went to great lengths to point out that he was only a man, and that he was basically agnostic anyway. The Hindu belief in God or many gods was one of the reasons that the Buddha rejected Hinduism as irrelevant, because there is no God in Buddhism. So, for me, it's not that Buddha had the wrong answers; he just wasn't helping with my questions. If I'm asking questions like, If there is a God…? there's not much point in trying to find out from someone who wasn't sure himself.

Hindus, Buddhists and reincarnation

After reading the primary sources it seemed to me that we are, in general, ignorant in the Western world of the real nature of Hindu and Buddhist beliefs concerning reincarnation. I believe Western society has unfairly distorted these religions without having checked the sources.

For instance, reincarnation is portrayed in the West as something desirable, yet according to the Hindus and Buddhists it is actually bad news. Their goal is to find true peace by *escaping* from the process of reincarnation. As the Buddhist teaching says:

...all birth into this world tends to ill not to ease.[6]

Reincarnation is the individual's penalty for sins. For example, it's possible for Buddhists to receive "an unfavourable rebirth" if they have ever "knowingly told a lie".[7] (If this is true I expect I'll be coming back as a tree in a dog pound.) Their goal is to avoid rebirthing. The "traveller" through life (or rather lives) aspires to reach Nirvana, and true peace, by eventually stopping himself or herself from being reincarnated. Meditation and yoga are the major means used to try and "abolish rebirth". (Yoga is the heart of Hinduism and means to yoke with the Hindu God Brahman.) The goal is to be released from the burden and attachments of this life and thus from rebirth.

Overall it seemed to me that the Western world has largely plagiarized and misused parts of the Hindu and Buddhist religions where it suits, without even understanding them.

The hills are alive with the sound of Muslims

One of the fastest-growing religions in Australia is that of Islam. I personally found the Koran straightforward to read. The founder of Islam, Mohammed, had visions of an angel in a cave in approximately AD 600. This forms the basis of the Muslim religion. Mohammed said these messages that he had been given by the angel had come from God. Mohammed acknowledged that there were other great prophets before him, such as Moses and Jesus, but he (Mohammed) was the last and greatest prophet, whose sayings superseded all others.

He had some limited knowledge of the Jewish and Christian religions and mentions them frequently. Things such as "The Jews say Ezra is the Son of God"[8] and that Christians believe in three Gods.[9] Reasonable mistakes for anyone to make if he had never read the Old and New Testaments. Perhaps harder to understand how "God" could have made such errors.

Jesus and the Jews

In my reading of the Hebrew and Christian texts (Old and New Testaments), one point of interest emerged. One that didn't necessarily answer any questions, but at least required further investigation.

Of all the major world religious leaders, only Jesus actually claimed to be God. (Just the same, I'm sure that if Buddha or Mohammed were around today they wouldn't be too happy to find that no one uses their name when they hit their thumb with a hammer.) Coming from a non-religious background, the idea that Jesus claimed to be God was something new to me. For one thing, I didn't realize that the claim to be the "Son of God" amounted to a claim to be God. I had always thought that the title "Son of God" was just expressing the idea "we are all sons and daughters of God". I know this sounds very ignorant to anyone who knows the basics of Christianity, which have been in place for the last 2,000 years, but I knew very little.

However, reading the Old and New Testaments from start to finish makes the matter much clearer. There are references in the Old Testament to the coming Messiah (or Christ). Such scriptures as Isaiah 9:6 say that this "son who will be born" is none other than "Mighty God". Now there is absolutely only one God in the doggedly monotheistic Jewish religion. When Jesus was born 750 years after this prophecy and grew up claiming to be the Son of God, there was no doubt in Jewish minds as to who he was claiming to be. In fact, Jesus' claim to be God was the reason he was crucified:

> **For this reason the Jews tried all the harder to kill him…he was even calling God his own Father, making himself equal with God.**[10]

The penalty for his "blasphemous" claim was death.

I've since found out that when ancient Jewish and even Oriental cultures used the term "Son of" in a theological context, it often meant "sameness of nature" or "equality of being".[11] For example, in the Old Testament "Son of the prophets" meant "a prophet".[12] Not that we needed to know this anyway, because it is obvious that both Jesus and the Jews who opposed him knew who he was claiming to be. In debate with these Jews, Jesus said:

> **"I and the father are one." Again the Jews picked up stones to stone him… "We are stoning you…for blasphemy because you, a mere man, claim to be God."**[13]

Rita, there are many other references that I could give you, but one of the clearest is where Jesus is called God outright. And how do you think Jesus responds? One of Jesus' disciples addresses him in awe as "My Lord and my God".[14] We need to set the scene here a little. This is not a 21st-century Western man dropping a swear word. To a devout first-century Jew this was about as profound a statement as could be made. Certainly, if Jesus had thought it was anything flippant or in any way breaking the third commandment (using God's name in vain), he would have rebuked the disciple. Rather, when his disciple called him God, Jesus commended him with the words:

Because you have seen me you have believed.[15]

The New Testament record leaves no doubt that Jesus and his followers claimed that he was God. There are dozens of instances. However, I wasn't content with only friendly records. What about the hostile witnesses of the times?

...for the hostile witness they had the witness box (maximum three rounds per juror)

The New Testament is not the only historical document from the first century and it's certainly not the only one that refers to Jesus. There are non-Christian and anti-Christian writers from the period, particularly Roman and Jewish historians, whom I also investigated.

How can any serious investigation ignore the testimony of

contemporary hostile witnesses? Modern theorists speculate on the history of Jesus while ignoring testimonies from contemporaries among whom were some of the greatest historians and public figures of the time. Though these writers were antagonistic towards Jesus and his movement, some were contemporaries of the writers of the New Testament and cannot be overlooked in any worthwhile study of the period.

One of the most significant Roman historians who lived in the first century was the administrator, and later Roman consul, Pliny the Younger. His collection of historical letters is described by the Encyclopedia Britannica as "intimately illustrating public and private life in the heyday of the Roman Empire". Pliny declares in his letter to the Emperor Trajan that he (Pliny) had ordered the execution of Christians, releasing only those whom he could force to "worship [the Emperor's] statue and the images of the gods". Those who refused were executed. He goes on to say that these Christians worshipped Christ as "a God".[16]

- SO, DAD, WHY DON'T WE HAVE MORE WRITINGS FROM ROMAN TIMES?
- WELL, SON, BECAUSE...ER...WELL, IT SEEMS THAT MOST OF THEM DIDN'T HAVE ANY ARMS.

27

Tacitus, Suetonius and Mara Bar-Serapion are other first-century anti-Christian historical writers who confirm significant details of the New Testament claims.

And later, Jesus' claim to deity also antagonized Jewish writers such as historian Rabbi Eliezer, who said that Jesus was one who dared to:

> …rise up and seek to make himself God and to cause the whole world to go astray… God is not a man that he should lie and if he says he is God he is a liar.[17]

The main point I noted in all this was that Jewish and Roman history, and anti-Christian writers (as well as Christian writers), confirm that Jesus and his followers claimed he was God. Rather than being 20th-century peddlers of a "latest theory", some of these writers were acclaimed historians, of whom some were actually contemporaries of Jesus' apostles.

All of which allows us, Rita, to reach our first logical step, a modest enough one, which we will call point B.

B: From both Christian and non-Christian sources, it is an undeniable fact that Jesus Christ claimed he was God.

Don't leave me this Waco

If we compare this claim of Jesus with other religious leaders we see significant contrast. *None* of the others claimed to be God. In fact, Mohammed, Confucius and Buddha all insisted they were only men. Apart from Jesus, the only people who have claimed to

28

be God were liars or madmen of little interest – men like the Wacko Waco cult leader David Koresh or Jonestown leader Jim Jones. No matter how many headlines such people make for a short time, history looks back on them as insignificant. We never did see the David Koresh Waco religion breaking out all over the world. Once Koresh was dead, that was the end of it. The cult leaders who deceive people clearly don't qualify as world religious leaders or teachers.

Follow the arguer

Initially this claim of Jesus may appear to be less significant than meets the eye. After all, it certainly doesn't prove he was God, only that he claimed to be God. We can only say we have got from point A to B.

However, a claim to deity, if it can be verified, relates directly to our original question. It needs to be followed up. If I am searching for a way through a forest and I find a paved road, I'm going to take it, at least until I find out how far it goes. If the road runs into a dead end, only then will I get off and head back into the trees. So if my search takes me in a particular direction from here, it is not because I want to ignore others. But that is where the investigation, at least temporarily, leads. Didn't Socrates exhort us to follow the argument wherever it leads? (Spare a thought for poor old Mrs Socrates.) At this point, then, the investigation has only these possibilities before it:

1. Jesus Christ was God (we'll call this point C).

Or

2. He was a liar or a lunatic (and I'm back in the forest again).

Telling a whopper?

Before we go on, let us look at whether there is some other middle way – a more comfortable way – of explaining Jesus Christ. For instance, what about the idea that he was just a great teacher?

Logic demands that if he was merely a great teacher but not really God, a great prophet but not really God, or anything else but not really God, then he must have been telling a whopper. After all, how can anyone be a great teacher or a great prophet and be lying about the most significant claim of all – that he was God?

To appreciate the magnitude of Jesus' claim we have to remember that this Orthodox Jew wasn't just claiming to be *any* God. He was claiming to be the God revealed in the Old Testament scriptures. This means he was claiming to be the *only* true God, a personal God rather than a "force", a God over all the world but independent from it, in total contrast to the pantheistic concept of God, where "part of God is in everyone".

It's this magnitude of Jesus' claim (and his intimate knowledge of Judaism) that makes it difficult to pass this off as either a "small fib" that got out of hand, or a politician's white lie "for the greater good". From the outset, Jesus' goal and teachings centred on his offering himself as "sinless", even offering all those who would follow him *life after death*. If these were lies, they were big from the start.

30

Clearly, if a man were to falsely claim to be God, he would either be an egomaniacal liar or have a hole in his marble bag. If Jesus was lying, he was not just any liar, but the biggest, most deceitful liar in the course of human history, deceiving more people than any other person in history, including a great many throughout the known world of his own time.

Nevertheless, history and logic demand that these are the only possibilities before us. Jesus was a liar or a lunatic, or he was God.

I thought I was so original with this logic, like maybe I had discovered something – only to find out that many people of far greater intellect than myself had already come to this same conclusion long before I had.

People who had started out as atheists, such as Oxford and Cambridge professor C.S. Lewis:

> I am trying here to prevent anyone saying the really foolish thing that people often say about him: I'm ready to accept Jesus as a great moral teacher but I don't accept his claim to be God. That is the one thing we must not say. A man who was merely a man and said the sort of things Jesus said would not be a great moral teacher. He would either be a lunatic on the level with the man who says he is a poached egg or else he would be the Devil of Hell. You must make your choice… You can shut him up for a fool, you can spit at him and kill him as a demon or you can fall at his feet and call him Lord and God. But let us not come with any patronising nonsense about his being a great human teacher. He has not left that open to us. He did not intend to.[18]

It may be "patronising nonsense" (apart from illogical), but it's still far more comfortable to stay where we are thus far with a good ol' "He was an important teacher but not really God". After all, how many people feel comfortable saying he was a liar? A lunatic? *Or* God?

But the difference is, Rita, that you and I are thrill-seekers. Comfort is for wussies, so we will move on!

The loon ranger?

In two thousand years Christianity has had some harsh critics, among them scholars and theologians, but I've not been able to uncover a single critic seriously proposing that Jesus was a lunatic.

In fact, from ancient scholars to modern psychiatrists, all agree that Jesus' teaching and character are the complete antithesis of an unstable mind. For example, psychiatrist James T. Fisher M.D. (though himself not a Christian) had this to say in his *Case Book of a Psychiatrist*:

> If you were to take the sum total of all the authoritative articles ever written by the most qualified of psychologists and psychiatrists on the subject of mental hygiene – if you were to combine them, and refine them, and cleave out the excess verbiage – if you were to take the whole of the meat and none of the parsley and if you were to have these unadulterated bits of pure scientific knowledge concisely expressed by the most capable poets, you would have an awkward and incomplete summation of [Jesus'] Sermon on the Mount.[19]

4

Once Upon a Tomb...

RETURN TO CINDER
I was sick of being "Elvis"
So I faked my death
They saw me lying, three days in state,
But I was just holding my breath
I heard someone say "cremation"
So I gave that coffin a shove
I weren't stickin' 'round in there to become
A hunka hunka burnin' love

E.P.

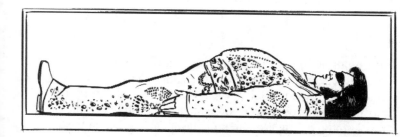

Serious scholarship (both for and against Christianity) rejects the view that Jesus could have been a lunatic. It will become clear why a "self-delusion" theory is not a possibility anyway. For now, we must examine each piece of evidence to help us decide between the two polar opposites:

Jesus was a liar or he was God.

It's worth noting that if we can show that Jesus told the smallest fib, we'll have exploded his claim to be God. In testing to see if he was telling the truth (point C), at least one thing is clear: historical information concerning Jesus is certainly extensive. As researcher Robert Morey puts it:

> There is more historical evidence for Jesus Christ than for any other historical person. There are literary works from his friends and foes, archaeological evidence, letters, correspondence and historians.[20]

Naturally, the more information available, the more completely we can test his integrity. Let's start with some basic historical facts and see what can be drawn from them.

Die for a lie?

First of all, Jesus Christ was in fact executed by way of crucifixion around the year AD 30. Here we are sticking to points that first-century non-Christian and *anti*-Christian historians verify. The Jewish historian Josephus recorded that Jesus did in fact die on a cross;[21] so too did the Roman pro-consul Tacitus, whom the

Encyclopedia Britannica calls "probably the greatest historian… who wrote in the Latin language". Tacitus confirms in his *Annals of Imperial Rome* that Christ was crucified by the governor of Judea, Pontius Pilate, during the reign of Tiberius.[22]

In any modern courtroom it would be thought ridiculous to hear evidence only from prosecution witnesses. But the evidence from non-Christian sources is such that even if the New Testament had never been written, Jesus' crucifixion could still be verified.

What is the significance of this? It is that Jesus, with nothing to gain if his story was a fake, refused to retract his claim to be God, even in the face of a peculiarly horrible death. A simple, "Oh but you misunderstand me", or "I meant we are all sons of God" could have saved his life (and yet at his trial, rather than any denial, he repeated the offence that sealed his fate).[23] Surely only a lunatic would carry on a hoax when there was nothing to gain from it but death by crucifixion. On the other hand, if his claim was true, he meant to die (see last chapter).

The fact that he actually died cannot reasonably be disputed. Apart from the non-Christian evidence (Roman and Jewish confirmation), there is the spear pushed through his side bringing forth water and blood.[24] Today's science confirms that this detail (recorded 2,000 years ago) is evidence of a dead body.

Moving a two-ton boulder – the origins of heavy rock 'n' roll?

The possibility that Jesus didn't actually die on the cross but was merely unconscious (known as the "swoon theory") was never postulated until the 19th century, at which time it was thoroughly refuted. The most convincing and complete refutation came from the world-renowned opponent of Christianity Dr D.F. Strauss. Although a prominent adversary of Christianity, Strauss devoted quite a large portion of the third volume of his work *Life of Jesus* to conceding that Jesus' death must have been a physical reality and an historical fact.

After all, how much "faith" do you need if you believe that Jesus survived what historians describe as the most horrific form of execution? Survived the nails through his hands and feet. Survived the collapse of his lungs as his limbs dislocated. Survived the spear through his side. Survived the tremendous loss of blood. Survived suffocation by the burial wrapping with approximately 100 lb of spices. Unwrapped himself. Pushed back a massive boulder. Tiptoed past the guards. Then fooled his followers into thinking he had triumphantly returned to life. Even if you did have enough faith to believe he could have survived all of this, you are left with a great liar and deceiver.

Those who have tried the hardest to "resuscitate" this swoon theory in recent times have fallen into an inevitable contradiction. Rather than admit that he would have had to be a liar (if he didn't really die), they actually still hold him up as a great moral teacher! But you just can't have your cake and eat it.

Nero – lifestyles of the rich and flamous

If Jesus went all the way to his death carrying out a self-deluded or deliberate fraud, then obviously he didn't come back from the dead.

That is why the "lunatic" or self-delusion theory fails. If he claimed to be God and was self-deluded, then the whole story would come to an abrupt end at his death, just as with any number of cult leaders. But here is where it only gets more complicated. Rather than ending at his death, in some ways it only begins. If his claims weren't true, we now have to add as liars or deluded the hundreds of people who claimed to have witnessed his resurrection from the dead. The penalty for maintaining this claim was often death. It's one thing to propose that Jesus was a liar, dying for a hoax, but we now have to imagine those claiming to be eyewitnesses to his resurrection also dying torturous deaths of execution just to keep the hoax going. On one occasion alone there were over 500 eyewitnesses. The first-century Roman historian Tacitus writes of the hatred for the "notoriously depraved Christians". (The Romans considered Christians to be depraved because they refused to worship the Roman gods.) Tacitus tells how Nero crucified Christians, dressed them in wild animal skins and allowed dogs to tear them to pieces, or paraded them on stakes as live burning torches to provide light for his own evening appearances.[25] Those martyrs claiming to be eyewitnesses to the resurrection would be dying these gruesome deaths while *knowing* it was a deception.

Among those who claimed to be eyewitnesses to the resurrected Jesus were many who were to write the New Testament. In fact, one of the qualifications to be an apostle of Jesus was that one had to have been an eyewitness before and after his resurrection.[26] These are the people from whom we get the biographical accounts and letters found in the New Testament. The apostle Peter's own testimony of having seen the glorified Jesus is:

We did not follow cleverly invented stories...but were eye-witnesses of [Jesus'] majesty.[27]

In other words, says Peter, "We're not makin' it up!" It's worth noting that these eyewitnesses were not especially brave "follow him to the death" people *before* Jesus was crucified. Not only did they scatter like cowards when he was arrested, but this same Peter had cursed and sworn he never even knew Jesus just to avoid his own arrest.[28] After the alleged resurrection, we see a different story. Something clearly transformed his resolve. Peter was crucified upside down, holding on to his testimony. Of the other apostles, only John died naturally; the rest went to horrible deaths by execution, crucifixion, the sword (James), beheading and so on. All because they wouldn't deny having seen a risen Christ. If the resurrection didn't happen, why were the apostles and others so determined to die for it? After all, plenty of people in history have died for something they believed in. But *no one* dies for something they *don't* believe in.

Author Josh McDowell set out as a sceptic to disprove the resurrection but eventually became convinced it was an historical fact. He points out that even if you include only the apostles, you would be hard pressed to find that many people in the whole of history who all willingly died for the same lie, while *knowing* it was a lie![29]

What about a mistaken identity? There are even people who claim to have seen Elvis alive. (Wasn't it the coroner who performed the autopsy who said that if Elvis wasn't dead when he got started, he was surely dead by the time he had finished?) But there is a tremendous difference here. The eyewitnesses to Jesus after the resurrection were not just reporting fleeting glimpses, as in "We saw Elvis in the car park". Rather, these eyewitnesses were people who knew Jesus and claimed intimate contact, having conversations and even eating meals with him during his resurrection appearances. Such detailed reports cannot be dismissed as merely mistaken: they must be either genuine or deliberate fabrication.

And this situation wasn't one of mass hysteria (like a "one in, all in") as with the Waco cult or Jonestown massacres, where questions still remain as to whether the events included suicide or murder. The followers of Christ were executed publicly and individually, at different places, and some even decades apart. Hardly the setting required for mass emotional and irrational action. For example, the martyrdom of Jesus' brother James in AD 62 is recorded in first-century *non-Christian* history by the Jewish historian Josephus. James had *not* been a follower of Jesus until he saw Jesus alive after the resurrection.[30] He eventually wrote one of the New Testament books. James was stoned to death for refusing to recant. He held on to his claim that he had seen the risen Christ.[31]

James was not the only sceptic to change his thinking dramatically after the resurrection. If we are looking to discredit the New Testament record on the grounds that "it was written only by hopeful supporters of Christ", then we are looking in the wrong place. One Roman citizen and a Jew of some high standing was among the greatest opponents of the first followers of Christ. He persecuted them with great zeal and brought many of them to trial and execution. There was a sudden change in his attitude after he claimed that he too had seen Jesus after his resurrection. This man, Paul of Tarsus, became the apostle to the Gentiles. He wrote more books of the New Testament than any other writer, and was eventually martyred himself for his belief when Nero cut off his head in about AD 67.

And all this for a lie?

Charles Colson – Nixon's watergoat

Charles Colson was U.S. President Richard Nixon's Special Counsel during the Watergate scandal. Colson became the scapegoat and went to prison for his part, while Nixon went free. Colson later became a Christian and says that one of the factors that convinced him was a comparison that he made between the Watergate affair and the resurrection. Watergate had been such a carefully planned lie, yet a few men couldn't keep the lid on the lie for even a few short weeks, and none of them had to go to their deaths to try and keep the lie going.

If we move into detail, the complications of Christ and his followers being all in on a hoax become enormous, as others have found:

"I CANNOT TELL A LIE... IT WAS CHARLES COLSON WHO CUT DOWN THE CHERRY TREE."

C.S. Lewis, who lectured in English Literature for almost 40 years at both Oxford and Cambridge Universities, said that there are only two possible views of the Gospels. Either they are reports of actual events or someone came up with the modern novel-writing technique over 1,500 years before anyone else.[32]

The sceptic is leaking!
(May the faucet be with you)

Here we could go into great details of the evidence for the resurrection, but this would require an encyclopedia to do it justice. There are those with far greater qualifications than myself who have detailed the evidence that I have examined. Many people, such as British trial lawyer Frank Morrison and author Lew Wallace (who wrote *Ben Hur*), have set out to refute the resurrection, but after complete examination have been convinced of its validity.

If you are questioning the resurrection seriously, then I suggest you examine works by people (more qualified than I) who have shown how strongly the evidence points to the resurrection as an historical fact. For example, in his book *The Resurrection, Proven Beyond Doubt*, Josh McDowell opens by saying:

> In my attempt to refute the resurrection I made nine acute observations of the resurrection that I had been totally unaware of. I had never realised there was so much positive historical, literary and legal testimony supporting its validity...[33]

McDowell had taken up a challenge to refute the resurrection while at university, and from his research he quotes the great German opponent of Christianity from the 19th century, D.F. Strauss. Despite his bitter opposition to Christianity, even Strauss realized the logical difficulty of both Jesus and his followers being in on a hoax together when he stated:

> The historian must acknowledge that the disciples firmly believed that Jesus was risen.[34]

The subject has been probed by some of the greatest legal minds:

> ...Dr Simon Greenleaf was more qualified to examine such evidence than any man who ever lived. He was the Royal Professor of Law at Harvard University and was declared by the chief Justice of the Supreme Court of the United States to be the greatest authority on evidence that could be quoted in any English speaking courtroom in the world. After writing voluminously on the laws of the legal evidences he decided to turn the searchlight of his knowledge of evidence and his ability to sift the true from the false toward the evidence for the resurrection of Christ.
>
> He examined each thread of evidence concerning the resurrection of Christ and concluded that in any unbiased courtroom in the world, if the evidence for the resurrection of Christ were presented it would be adjudged to be an absolute historical fact. This was the opinion of the greatest authority

on evidence that the world has ever known, Dr Simon Greenleaf of Harvard.[35]

Quotes such as these need to be examined in context to be fully appreciated and are not presented here as evidence in themselves. Nevertheless there are so many people qualified in law and historical disciplines who have come to the same conclusion after examining the evidence (despite some of them starting out with an antagonistic view). See the following few other examples I came across:

- Lord Caldecote, Lord Chief Justice of England
- Professor Thomas Arnold, author of *History of Rome*, holder of the Chair in Modern History at Oxford
- Dr J.N.D. Anderson, British legal expert
- Dr Edwin M. Yamauchi, Associate Professor of History at Miami University
- Walter M. Chandler, Former Justice of the New York State Supreme Court
- Ben C. Hillard, Chief Justice of Colorado State Supreme Court.

5

Did ancient writers get R.S.I.? (Retirement Scheme Injury)

The next point I will discuss is the accuracy or preservation of the original text of the New Testament. I think it is important to test its reliability as a document since we are interested in examining the truth of its claims.

The first thing that struck me about the New Testament was the fact that it was largely written by eyewitnesses, people who were actually there at the time. Much of it was written in the form of letters. Whether the writers were telling the truth or lying about what they saw and heard, one thing is certain: they weren't telling handed-down legends.

But how do we know we are reading, unchanged, what they wrote? In his book *The Ten Wonders of the Bible*, Don Stewart addresses this point:

> Since we possess so many manuscripts we can be assured the original text has been preserved. We never have to revert to guessing to determine what the original text said.[36]

I will elaborate on this "volume" of manuscripts shortly, but the question of accuracy must have been a concern even from the first century. As Dr Charles V. Taylor points out:

> Early Church writers often appealed to the fact that anyone can consult holders of the correct form of text, even if no autograph is available. An orthodox believer called Gaius in about 180 AD named four heretics, saying they couldn't deny their guilt because they couldn't produce originals for their copies. This suggests that some could produce the original wording.[37]

This is important. It was taken for granted that manuscripts could be verified, which could prevent people from getting away with changing the wording. In fact we even have small portions of the New Testament in existence today that predate this period. There are parts of a manuscript dated AD 125 sitting in the John Rylands Library in Manchester, England. The schoolyard tale that I used to believe was that "everybody knows that the Bible was written centuries after the facts". That one still makes the rounds today, but the evidence to the contrary is sitting there and is not going anywhere.

Then there are quotations from the early Church Fathers, such as Clement of Rome. Writing in about AD 95, Clement quotes the gospels and other letters of the New Testament. This shows that these had been widely circulated well before this time, when at least the apostle John was still alive. This leaves the idea of a late date for the New Testament impossible – unless Clement and others were quoting the New Testament writers via mental telepathy, since they would have to be quoting things that had not yet been written.

If the New Testament is really what it claims to be (i.e. the inspired word of God), then you would expect it to have been preserved accurately. From a literary and manuscript standpoint, the only way you can really appreciate how overwhelming the evidence is in this area is by comparison with other historical literature. The criteria that scholars apply to test the accuracy of ancient manuscripts fall into two main areas:

1. The time span from when the work was originally written to the time of the oldest currently available manuscript.
2. The number of manuscripts.

In test no. 1, the shorter the time span between the writer's lifetime and the age of the oldest currently available manuscript, the less possibility there is of a corruption in copying. As for test no. 2, the larger the number of manuscripts, the more sources (or "witnesses" as they are called), and the easier it is to check the accuracy of copying. These are the two main tests scholars use, so let's see how the New Testament stacks up against other ancient historical records.

WORK	WHEN WRITTEN	EARLIEST COPY	TIME SPAN	NO. OF COPIES
Caesar	100–44 BC	AD 900	1,000 years	10
Plato	427–347 BC	AD 900	1,200 years	7
Thucydides	460–400 BC	AD 900	1,300 years	8
Herodotus	480–400 BC	AD 900	1,300 years	8
New Testament	AD 40–100	AD 125	25 years	24,000 (5,000 Greek)[38]

There is no comparison with other literature, religious or secular, in the whole of history. It's no wonder so many literary scholars have concluded that if the New Testament were a secular document its accuracy would not even be questioned. Rylands' Professor at Manchester University, England, the late Dr F.F. Bruce, looked at the scrutiny placed on the New Testament compared to other ancient literature and commented:

> …no classical scholar would listen to an argument that the authenticity of Herodotus or Thucydides is in doubt because the earliest manuscripts are over 1,300 years later than the originals.[39]

Renowned scholar Sir Fredrick Kenyon says of the New Testament:

> No other ancient book has anything like such early and plentiful testimony to its text, and no unbiased scholar would deny that the text that has come down to us is substantially sound.[40]

Romeo and Julius?

The writings of Shakespeare handed down within a 200-year period have over 100 variant readings, many of

ANCIENT SPELLING ERROR MAY YET UNCOVER HISTORICAL WRITER BEHIND PLATO.

which materially affect the outcome of the manuscripts. In the 2,000 years during which the New Testament has been handed down, no manuscript has ever been uncovered with any variant reading that has ever contradicted New Testament doctrine. As scientist Henry Morris points out:

> The written records of Christian origins are in this respect available in far greater variety and antiquity than are those of any other personages or happenings in the whole world prior to the invention of printing.[41]

The Dead Sea Scrolls –
you ain't Essene nothin' yet

Not all the writings of the Essene community, discovered in the famous Dead Sea Scrolls, were religious, but one of the first books discovered in 1947 was a complete manuscript of Isaiah (Old Testament book written approximately 750 BC). This manuscript, dated at about 100 BC, was older than those previously held by about 1,000 years. Naturally there was great curiosity as to how much the later copies of Isaiah would vary from those of 1,000 years earlier.

There was also special interest in speculation that prophecies in the book of Isaiah (particularly those concerning the Christ or Messiah) had been added in over the centuries to support Christian doctrine. When compared with the unreliability of other ancient literature, it is quite incredible that, after examination, the content of the book of Isaiah was found to have been preserved over those 1,000 years.

Coincidence? An ancient book that claims to be the inspired word of God is also the book that (unlike other ancient literature) survives with content intact?

We all know how easily a story changes when we whisper to one another around a circle.... How easily human error can change things. The Bible went to three different continents over the early centuries and one might have expected it to be in a mess now. Yet against all normal expectations it has survived with all essential content unchanged to the present day.

The "coincidences" continue to add up.

Archaeology – *take this job and shovel it!*

Archaeology has confirmed the New Testament to such a degree of accuracy that secular archaeologists use it as a guide map in their work. In examining the archaeological claims of the Bible, author Don Stewart quotes world-famous archaeologist Nelson Glueck:

It may be stated categorically that no archaeological discovery has ever controverted a biblical reference.[42]

Another world-famous archaeologist, John Romer, makes no secret of his being non-Christian. He was used by *60 Minutes* to do an exposé on radical theologian Barbara Thiering. Standing in the actual sites in Jerusalem, Romer was able to show that, from an archaeological perspective, the New Testament account "…accurately describes this environment. The flowers and the trees and the lake…" He even pointed out such details as the actual steps Jesus climbed to enter Jerusalem for his trial.

Romer's presentation was impressive and exposed the lack of credibility of Thiering's theories from an archaeological and historical perspective. Nevertheless, Romer's attitude was a reminder that people often try not to think too deeply about the implications of evidence. Here was Romer the archaeologist admitting where the evidence was leading, but Romer the man was indifferent to it. After he had pointed out what he said were the remains of the actual tomb where Jesus was buried, Romer was asked by the reporter what happened to Jesus after he was crucified. Unable to contradict all he had said about the accuracy of the New Testament, Romer could only laugh and say, "Perhaps he rose from the dead after three days." [43]

Raiders of the lost archaeology

There have always been critics who have assumed that biblical events must be regarded as myth until archaeology has verified them. What each generation overlooks is that this kind of criticism has consistently failed century after century with each new discovery of *actual evidence*.

For example, even up until recent times the "existence" of the New Testament figure Pontius Pilate (who ordered the execution of Jesus) was questioned by archaeologists. Why? Not because there was contrary evidence, but because archaeology had not yet found corroboration. However, in 1961 an archaeological excavation in Caesarea uncovered proof not only of Pilate's existence, but also that he was in fact Prefect of Judea. As archaeologist John Elder stated:

> The overall result is indisputable. Forgotten cities have been found, the handiwork of vanished peoples has reappeared, contemporary records of biblical events have been unearthed… Nowhere has archaeological discovery refuted the Bible as history.[44]

Let's move on.

6

How to lose a prophet

To try and test point C (Jesus was not lying but told the truth in his claim to be God), I think it's important also to examine Jesus' claim that the Bible is the inspired word of God. If the Bible doesn't stack up, then Jesus' claim is discredited.

In biblical times false prophecy was considered a great crime. One test to see if someone was inspired by God was to test their ability to predict the future. If anyone claimed to be a prophet but made a single incorrect prediction they were "stoned" as a false prophet. (Too bad we don't have this now: it might make a few of those Melbourne weather forecasters get their act together.) I'll now quote from Dr D. James Kennedy:

> There are over 2,000 specific prophecies in the Bible which have already been fulfilled. This is particularly astounding when we recall that there are no such prophecies in the "scripture" of any other religion... These biblical prophecies deal with almost every nation and scores of cities with which Israel had some dealings.
>
> It cannot be said that these prophecies were written after the events for many of the events took place hundreds or even thousands of years after the prophecy was made. Nor can it be said that they are vague or obscure, because they are highly

specific in their details. Nor can it be said that they are merely lucky guesses because there are over 2,000 of them which have infallibly come to pass. Nor can it be said that these were the things which were likely to take place because they were indeed extremely unlikely events.[45]

I won't write a whole "book" listing all the prophecies here, because there are others who have done that. However, when you think of over 2,000 often detailed prophecies all coming to pass, if we are being fair, surely the burden of proof has been shifted to the prosecution (those who say Christ was lying). How can you explain that mere human beings could possibly be 100% accurate over 2,000 times? Let me cite Professor J.P. Free, quoted from a non-religious book called *Predictions*, which examines futuristic predictions in history:

> There are over 332 distinct predictions in Hebrew scriptures that were fulfilled in Jesus. Among the forecasts were the birth of Jesus in Bethlehem. (Micah 5:2)[46]

Nostradamus – apparently he was very unpredictable

The non-religious book on predictions that the above quote was taken from showed that the Bible stood alone as an infallible predictor, particularly when it was compared with the great non-biblical prophets such as Nostradamus.

The authors recorded 354 events from Nostradamus' writings

53

that were treated as predictions, of which only 16 could be considered vaguely correct. Of course those 16 are the ones always paraded on the TV specials. But even if we accept those 16, Nostradamus' accuracy is still less than 5% (I'm beginning to wonder if Nostradamus really even had a hunched back).

– I PREDICT THAT YOU WILL BECOME A RICH MAN VERY SOON.
– THAT'S AMAZING, MR NOSTRADAMUS...BY THE WAY, STICK 'EM UP AND GIMME ALL YOUR MONEY!!!

If a 5% accuracy rate qualifies one as a great prophet, how do we view the Bible, which has over 2,000 predictions with 100% accuracy, 332 of which were fulfilled in Jesus himself?

Let's look at just four of the significant biblical prophecies concerning the Messiah. Today many Jews are still waiting for a Messiah who will be:

PROPHECY	WHEN WRITTEN
The Son of God (Isaiah 9:6)	750 BC
Born in Bethlehem (Micah 5:2)	700 BC
Crucifixion, pierced hands and feet (Psalm 22:16)	1000 BC
Descendant of King David (Jeremiah 33:15)	600 BC

These are just four of more than 300 prophecies from the Old Testament that describe the coming Messiah. They were written centuries before Jesus was born and yet it is him they describe and no other person who ever lived.

54

The prophetic words in Psalm 22:16–18 describe details of Jesus' future crucifixion:

> *…a band of evil men has encircled me, they have pierced my hands and my feet…People stare and gloat over me. They divide my garments among them and cast lots for my clothing.*

One especially impressive aspect of this prophecy is that it was written at a time (1000 BC) when crucifixion had not been invented as a form of execution. Crucifixion came into vogue in about the 6th century BC.

One of the things that also defies a "coincidence" theory is that some of the 2,000 prophecies were predicted more than once by different authors centuries apart.

The idea of 40 authors of the 66 books of the Bible collaborating over 1,500 years and sometimes doubling up on "lucky guesses", without getting any wrong, is far-fetched to say the least.

Jewish origins

If there are so many detailed prophecies about the Messiah, why didn't the Jews accept Jesus?

Quite a few did! Thousands were converted within a short space of time.[47] These Jews were the first Christians. The earliest Christian Church was made up of Jews who were trying to convert Gentiles, not the other way around. Jesus gave a great commission to his *Jewish* followers, telling them to spread their message to all the nations (Gentiles).[48] Christianity didn't originate as a Gentile religion. It was a Jewish religion. It was radical in that it not only accepted Gentiles, but also actively sought to convert them.

But what about today?

There are approximately 17 million Jews in the world today and many take great pride in their heritage, but very few are strictly practising religious Jews. When compared to the number of religious Jews, the number of Jewish Christians, while still an obvious minority, is quite notable. Today's Christian Jews are called Messianic Jews, since they believe that Jesus is the Messiah. They include international Christian groups such as *Jews for Jesus*.

Many of these Messianic Jews are among the most learned Christians when it comes to historical and biblical evidence for the Christian faith, including defending Jesus as their Messiah. This is understandable, considering the stigma and persecution involved in making such a commitment. Naturally they would want to be sure of their facts.

But Jesus as the Jewish Messiah is not so radical. In fact, without him Judaism is left with some unsolved riddles. For example, there was a key promise given at the beginning of the Jewish nation. It was given to the very first Jew, Abraham (Abram, as he was then known). At Abraham's initial calling, the promise was that God would make Abraham and his descendants into a great nation, and through him all the nations of the earth would be blessed.[49] Now with all due respect to Woody Allen, we might ask the question: "How have all nations of the earth been blessed through the Jews?" On its own it seems like a far-fetched prophecy. But think about it in the light of the great commission that Jesus gave to his first Jewish followers, "…go and make disciples of *all nations*…" [50] Two thousand years later, with the message of Jesus over almost the entire globe, one of the primary complaints against Christianity is, "Why do Christians think they have to go and bother *every nation*…?" The answer from Jesus is that his message carries blessing for all who hear and believe in him. [51]

I found it particularly interesting listening to a Messianic Jew from Israel speak on his conversion. He kept pointing to the Old Testament prophecies about the Messiah, saying that he saw no alternative but to "believe". He thought it inconceivable that hundreds of prophecies about Jesus could just be coincidences.

In fact the "coincidences" continue to build.

The story is told about a non-believing Jew who denied to a Christian friend his own religion, saying he did not believe the miracles of the Old Testament. The friend found this so ironic because this man's very existence as a Jew was a miracle in itself. After all, the Old Testament predicted that the Jews would be dispersed from their land. In addition, God promised that the nation of Israel would be maintained and eventually restored to their own land, which was fulfilled in Israel's return from exile in Babylon. [52]

Today the survival of the Jewish nation is still unique in the world, considering all the persecutions they have suffered. In 1948 the land of Israel became a State. In 1967 Israel captured Jerusalem, and the Jewish people held that land as a free people for the first time since the Babylonians captured Judah in 586 BC. Hundreds of nations have been dispersed throughout history, but none of these have maintained their nation and national identity in the long term and they certainly haven't returned to their own land after being established in other foreign countries.

You may already know of the international understanding that allows Jews to maintain citizenship of Israel while living in foreign countries. I rang the Jewish consulate in Melbourne and they told me how governments often "turn a blind eye for us". For some unexplained reason, many countries that don't normally allow dual citizenship make an exception to allow Jews to become citizens, whilst retaining their Israeli citizenship. The consulate staff also told me that, unlike other nations, when a Jew who has never lived in Israel "returns" to Israel, he or she is granted "citizenship on arrival", without any residential waiting period as with other countries. The Jewish nation is maintained in a miraculous way even today.

And yet it is true that the majority of Jews did not accept Jesus as their Messiah. Ironically, if it had been any other way, it would have been inconsistent with Israel's own history. One read of the Old Testament shows a people constantly in rebellion against their God and rejecting each prophet that God sent them. Despite this, in mercy, God in the Old Testament promised that he would still preserve a faithful remnant of the nation of Israel (Isaiah 10:22). The promise to save a remnant is not inconsistent with what is unfolding.

But let's not be too hasty in asking, "Why didn't the Jews see Jesus as the Messiah if the prophecies are there?" The same question could be put to 21st-century Gentiles. Don't Gentiles have every bit as much access to the same evidence and prophecies? The Gentiles are no different from Jews. Whether it's the first century or the 21st century, Jew or Gentile, the evidence has been available, but there is another agenda. (We'll get to that later.)

The earth is round –
Lucy in the sky with a camera?

My next step in testing the integrity of the Bible and the credibility of its record of Jesus is to consider the state of its scientific knowledge.

In his book *Many Infallible Proofs*, scientist Henry Morris points out dozens of Bible verses that assume facts about the physical universe (in fields such as hydrology, geology, astronomy, meteorology, biology and physics), facts that were simply unknown to scientists until thousands of years later.[53] Rita, if the Bible isn't inspired, as Jesus claims it to be, you've got to ask how its writers could have known all these things before science discovered them. For example, how could the prophet Isaiah have known?

A Round Earth!
He sits enthroned above the circle of the earth and its people are like grasshoppers.[54]

The New Wilson's Hebrew Dictionary (of Old Testament words) says that the "literal English meaning" of the word rendered "circle" in this quote (from Isaiah 40:22) is *circle* or *sphere*.

W.E. Jackel says of this ancient scripture:

Writing to refute the theory of the antipodes, a learned divine of the day declared "Is there any man so silly as to believe that men exist having their feet above their heads, trees with their fruit hanging downward, rain hail and snow falling upward?"[55]

How could they have known the earth was round 2,700 years ago? It's obvious that the idea conflicted with the science of the day and with other ancient writings, including other religious writings.

The Muslims' Koran says that Allah created the earth flat,[56] and the Hindu scriptures describe the earth not only as a flat triangle, but as held up by giant elephants who are standing on the backs of giant turtles swimming in a giant pool. The Buddhist scriptures even give us the names of the elephants. Mahapadma holds up the world in the south.[57]

Contrast that with the knowledge of the Bible: it says not only that the earth is round, but that it's suspended in space.[58] There are many instances where the Bible's understanding of the physical world is ahead of scientific discovery. The God of the Bible even asks Job if he has walked in the recesses of the deep or journeyed to springs under the sea.[59] Modern equipment reveals freshwater springs under the deepest seas. Another coincidence?

Ancient Jewish regulations – *Jurassic pork*

Even Jewish laws from the Old Testament that relate to religious ceremony have been found to reflect medical and health concerns that we associate only with 19th- and 20th-century science. For example, the hygiene value of laws in the book of Leviticus (for quarantining the diseased "outside the camp" and the extensive "washing" required after handling a dead body) wasn't recognized until the 19th century. It was then discovered by Dr Ignaz Semmelweiss that doctors handling the dead and then delivering babies (without washing hands) led to higher infant mortality rates. Semmelweiss was ridiculed by his peers as a fanatic before the importance of his discovery was recognized.[60]

The Bible is not written as a scientific textbook, nor are Jewish laws meant to be a handbook on health tips. The purpose of those laws was to teach the people that they were to be set apart as holy. But, indirectly, the Bible abounds with insights into the natural world that go unrecognized until science gives us the eyes to see them.

7
Unknowable?

We have assessed a certain amount of evidence and it's now possible to review the progress we have made. Dare I say that the case for Jesus being God (as opposed to a liar) is *not* built on "faith" alone, but is backed by some pretty convincing evidence. Rather, the case against him (that logically must accept he was a liar or lunatic) would seem to require a good deal more "faith".

Try to really stand in the shoes of both sides of this issue and ask yourself which side really has more going for it in the way of tangible evidence? If you reject Jesus' claim to be God, you must accept that Jesus was a liar or a lunatic (whether that feels comfortable or not), and that Bible accuracy and prophecies are all a series of massive coincidences. But which way did the evidence really point – Jesus as liar or as God?

I can't pretend I've given you an autographed photo from heaven, but I do believe I've given you more to go on than many everyday things you would consider to be proven facts. All I'm saying is that, utilizing historical evidence, I've made it from point A to B and B to C, even if I haven't got all the details in between that you might like.

When I have shown people in religious cults documentation that exposes their organization as fraudulent, there is often a common initial reaction. No matter how convincing the evidence is, they find one minor point to criticize and hold on to it, as if that somehow makes everything else disappear. My point is that even if you can find something to criticize in my presentation, the big picture is that we still have to deal with this historical figure from the first century who claims to be God and who asks each one of us:

But what about you, who do you say that I am?[61]

In other words, there may still be some remaining unanswered questions. There may even be some questions that cannot be answered. But the real issue is, do any of these unanswered questions provide grounds for turning Jesus into a liar? If not, then we have moved from A through B to C.

The trap – *it's so easy to fall in, Love*

The difficulty is that even if you find the evidence convincing, there are consequences that go beyond the intellectual exercise. If Jesus was telling the truth, then according to his teaching, being "for or against him" becomes the single most important question in life.

Some who agree with the evidence quickly pass over it and go back to their personal philosophical ideas of the "God I would like to believe in" or "not believe in". Or, because they don't "feel" any different, they casually accept that he wasn't a liar but still: "it doesn't do anything for me, but it's okay for you". Here my request is that you don't pass over the logical facts. It's not a question of this being something that *appeals* to me or to you. There is no escaping the fact that Jesus Christ was either a monumental liar, or he is God.

I felt a great piercing sensation in my heart! (Turned out my new shirt had one pin left)

Perhaps the gravity of being able historically and logically to conclude Jesus was not a liar doesn't "grab you" or provide some "spiritual awakening", but if you're waiting for some kind of "feeling" or "experience" to accompany such a conclusion, then you might be waiting for ever.

No matter how many fine Christians there are who can relate testimonies of feelings they had before or after conversion, there is no appeal in the New Testament to your feelings. The only appeal is to cold, hard facts and to "keep your head in all situations".[62] I don't say this to diminish the importance of feelings, only to point out that fatal mistakes have been made by those who think only with their feelings.

Unlike facts, feelings can be unreliable. The facts have been laid out in history and have always been sitting there. There's no big secret. I haven't discovered anything new. Despite different opinions and new "theories" on what happened to Jesus, even a Mr Potato-Head like me was able to simply walk into the National Library and read such things as the Roman Tacitus' record of the crucifixion of Christ under Pontius Pilate. It's really not just the facts that are important, but our reaction to them. How do we deal honestly with these facts?

64

Sitting on the fence still leaves you with a bottom line

Thinking expert and prolific author Edward de Bono summed up the attitude of Jesus so well in his book *I Am Right, You Are Wrong*. De Bono said that Jesus is one of those narrow people who insists on using logic and "makes no allowance for neutrals".[63] De Bono cites as an example of this, Jesus' statement in Matthew 12:30:

He who is not with me is against me.

Edward is no de Bono-head. He has seen through the whole thing. Rita, all this time we thought it was those Christians who were intolerant, but really they were just being true to their teacher. Jesus himself is the "intolerant" one! Obviously he didn't leave room for fence-sitting if he says those who are not for him are against him.

You may begin to understand why I laboured the point that the only real possibilities concerning Jesus are that he was either a liar or God (even though very few people, including yourself, have ever suggested he was a liar). I did this because, according to *Jesus himself*, if you sit on the fence or take a "non-decisive" stance, it's the same as calling him a liar anyway. You may be sitting there thinking, "Well I would *never* say that Jesus was a liar". But indifference is a statement in itself. If you introduce yourself to someone as Rita from Melbourne and that person responds indifferently, saying, "Well maybe you are – maybe you aren't;

I don't know", what would you say to that? You might respond with… "Well, are you calling me a liar?" How much more would Jesus, in his claim, expect to be taken at his word? You might not have consciously thought of Jesus as a liar, but that is the position you take if you don't believe he is God. Whether you have thought it through is irrelevant – that is your logical position or the "side of the fence" you sit on.

Procrastination (I think this means I'm *for* crastination, but I never got around to finding out)

It's amazing how many people make decisions in life by making a "non-decision". Ignoring something in the hope it will go away. The overweight guy who is told by his doctor to exercise but never gets around to it until he has a heart attack. The guy who stays in a job he hates for 40 years but never really does anything about it.

The non-decision has a certain comfort for a time, but is in effect a decision too – it has to be lived with (or died with). We are just as responsible for things we *don't* do. If Christ was lying, then none of this really matters. But if he wasn't, then it could hardly matter more.

A good picture of "ignoring" things is the story of the guy on a lake with each of his feet in two separate rowing boats. One of the boats has large holes in it and is sinking; the other boat is good. The trouble is, as long as he continues to keep one foot in each boat, he's still going to end up in the water!

Phantom of the op shop

Rita, don't settle for anything second-hand. To make an informed decision about Jesus' claims, you need to read the New Testament yourself. The old "I read it when I was a kid" doesn't count any more than if you had read Shakespeare "as a kid" and expected to have a true understanding of his work.

It amazes me that most people have an opinion of Jesus and yet hardly any of them have ever actually read the New Testament. Even many who are familiar with different portions, or verses out of context, haven't actually read it through. And yet the New Testament is only about 250 pages long, which is no longer than a novel.

How embarrassing it would be if a journalist or critic had reviewed or given an opinion on a book, and it was later discovered they had not even read it! And yet no one seems too embarrassed about giving an uninformed opinion on Jesus and the New Testament.

They used to call me level-headed – now it's just blockhead

Well, Rita, it all started out so cool. I was a guy studying all the religions. That's pretty cool to most people. Sort of "intellectual", as long as you don't get too involved or come to any conclusions.

But after I finished, I realized that I personally had to conclude that there is no way Jesus Christ was a liar, and there are consequences that go along with that if you're honest about it. But wait a minute! That means Christianity, doesn't it? All of sudden I'm not so cool. Oh bother! If only I'd decided on Buddhism, or started meditating, or at least bought one of those floatation tanks or something. At least that's cool in a mystical sort of way. But Christians! They're the guys I used to make fun of in my stand-up routines. I've given Christianity a hard time in front of thousands of people.

But whether it's cool or not, I didn't choose the evidence.

It's a little like when you first realized that your parents really had to be more than just good friends. Sooner or later you have to accept the reality (that you just weren't consulted as to whether you "liked" the idea or thought it was "cool").

This investigation initially looked for logical ways to test questions about God. Eventually we were testing someone who claimed be God. I extensively tested Jesus. Should I have spent more time on the other religions?

How the West was wondering

Don't let your Western ignorance of non-Christian religions betray you. There is no criticism or avoiding of other religions in putting only Jesus to this test. Why? Because of *all* the other major world religious leaders in history, including Buddha, Mohammed, Zoroaster, etc.:

- *None* of them ever claimed to be God.
- *None* of them claimed to know God personally.
- *None* of them claimed they could give eternal life.

- *None* of them claimed to be able to grant forgiveness at a future judgment (even though they all believed in a future judgment).
- *None* of them claimed their teaching was meant for all peoples of all nations, in all ages.

It's for this reason that I say my study of all religions led to one.

Reindeer droppings keep falling on my head

I don't want you to complain that I skimmed over the other religions. I didn't. I studied them. But if you want a more detailed appraisal you will have to wait for a "Volume 2". In fact, I began with more doctrinal comparisons only to edit them out, for two main reasons. Firstly, a complete analysis of comparative religious doctrines would make this into an encyclopedia. Secondly, and more importantly, comparing doctrines (Christian, Buddhist, etc.) would have added nothing to our search.

You might have found such a comparison interesting. You may even have found a preference based on your personal taste or cultural influences. But would "personal taste" provide us with any tangible or objective test? We might as well make up our own religious doctrines. How about a belief that Santa Claus will literally fly those reindeer down from the North Pole one of these Christmases? Who is to say otherwise? No, Rita, religious doctrines themselves don't offer anything objective to test. Doctrines become important only when we have found an independent objective reason to believe they are true.

Play it again, Saddam

Most of us think of those "afterlife" questions as unanswerable. This may be so from a scientific point of view, because they can't be physically observed. However, they can be tested from a legal and historical perspective. For example, here are two historical facts. Captain James Cook discovered Australia in 1770, and in 2003 Saddam Hussein led Iraq in war. These are facts, but they are not scientific facts. For something to be a fact of science it has to be able to be repeated and tested under observation, and that's impossible. Film footage of Saddam doesn't prove anything: it might have been a fake. If you want a scientific fact, you have to repeat it under observation. So does that make the truth of these events meaningless? No. We know that these things in both distant past and short-term past really happened. Things can still be tested and even proven from a legal and historical perspective, when eyewitnesses leave a record of events.[64] In the same way, Christianity can be tested because it has its basis in historical events and people.

Ah-ha, I hear you say! Historical and legal evidence can sometimes fail to give an accurate verdict. In fact, Australia's most famous legal case proves just that. Do you remember the Lindy Chamberlain case? (Even the Americans heard of us when Meryl Streep played Lindy in the movie version.) Lindy claimed a dingo carried off and killed her baby, Azaria. The prosecution claimed Lindy murdered her baby. She was found guilty and subsequently jailed. Years later the case was overturned. The historical and legal evidence failed to deliver the correct answer. However, I put it to you that historical and legal evidence is limited and unreliable *only when the testimony itself is limited.*

The strength of Lindy's testimony was limited because she was the only eyewitness. But what if there had been other eyewitnesses who claimed that they had seen the baby taken and killed by a dingo?

In fact, let's suppose there had been over 500 people who claimed to have seen the dingo take and kill Azaria.

And what if among these eyewitnesses were many who knew Azaria and could identify her specifically as the baby taken?

And what if among the eyewitnesses were many who were willing to go to their deaths rather than retract their testimony, saying that they saw a dingo kill Azaria?

And what if among the eyewitnesses were actual enemies of Lindy Chamberlain, people who wanted nothing more than to see Lindy put behind bars, and yet were still willing to go to their own deaths, and were in fact executed for not retracting their testimony?

If this had been the case, wouldn't we have said that Lindy Chamberlain's innocence was proven beyond reasonable doubt? In fact wouldn't we have said it was *a proven fact beyond any doubt?*

Well, take another look. It's the same evidence that we have for the case of Jesus.

The only difference would be the time factor, but I put it to you that this is another point in *favour* of the Jesus case. Time has a great way of sorting out error – emotions can dominate in the heat of the moment, but viewing the facts with hindsight is far more objective. Most Australians who are old enough to remember the Lindy Chamberlain case can look back with embarrassment.

71

Emotions ran so high at the time. Nearly all of the country presumed this woman guilty of murdering her own baby – with no motive whatsoever and no decisive evidence against her. Time has calmed the emotional storm and given a more objective view. And how has the case of Jesus stood the test of time?

Jesus' case has been battered with a more rigorous testing (over 2,000 years) than any other event in the history of the world – and it still stands firm.

We question the strength of the historical method in situations where testimony is limited. But when there are a number of people testifying to an event that involves a matter of life and death, there is a certainty to it. You just can't rewrite history. Let's take, for example, the revisionist historian David Irving. He attempted to rewrite the history of the holocaust. Do you remember how years ago he was refused a visa to even enter Australia? What happened to freedom of speech? If he has an opinion on history, why not let him give it? Well, it was not just a question of freedom of speech. What he had to say wasn't just offensive on an emotional level. It was offensive on an intellectual level. The fact is that it was just too easy to prove that what he claimed was not true.

How can it be proved that he was wrong? After all, the events of the Second World War happened back in the first half of the last century. That's a long time ago.

But long ago as it was, there are people still alive today who can say, "I was there! I know what happened. David Irving is wrong!" Or there are many of the next generations who could say, "My parents were there! My grandparents were there!"

Irving might be able to gather together enough people to have a bit of a Nazi-party, but you can't rewrite history. Not when you have that much weight of testimony. For the same reason, Christianity would never have got off the ground if the events were false. Unlike every other religion, Christianity did not begin with doctrines or private spiritual encounters; it began with historical events. These events were not done in a corner. They were public. The gospel accounts of the New Testament were being widely circulated much closer to the time of the events than our comparison with David Irving and last century's Second World War. Think about that. Irving's theories are going nowhere with serious historians. If the description of events recorded in the New Testament had been falsified or even exaggerated it too would have gone nowhere. There would have been too many people to say, "I was there!" "This stuff is not true." "He never claimed that." Or the next generation would have said, "Well we checked with those 500 people who are supposed to have seen the resurrected Jesus, and they said it was not true." The momentum would have screamed to a halt – especially when people had to die if they wanted to hold on to it.

Well, Rita, we can't rewrite history just because we don't like it. The facts are staying where they are and the historical method needs to be examined on its merits.

Foundation

Remember, we said at the beginning that the only way we could know anything for certain is if we had a source completely outside of ourselves to give us the great answers. A source not reliant on our limited and fallible experiences. We determined that this ultimate source would have to be no one less than God himself! We have looked at evidence for Jesus' credibility in his own claim to be that very God. We really need to pause for a moment to contemplate, "Where does this take us?"

While we have looked at external evidence for the reliability of the Bible, there is an internal element that is crucial. If Jesus is the outside source of infallible truth, then the big question is: what is *Jesus'* attitude toward the Bible? Was he even concerned, let alone aware, that his words were to be recorded? Are we expected to believe that the Bible is true simply because Christians *say* it is?

I don't want you to miss this. We are definitely *not* relying on the opinions of Christians as to whether the Bible is the word of God. The truth of the Bible has no less a guarantor than Jesus himself. He is the one we need to deal with. It was Jesus who said that the scripture cannot be broken.[65] But what if the apostles had wanted to slip in a few ideas of their own? It was Jesus who said that the writers of the New Testament would be guided into all truth by God's Spirit.[66] So was Jesus anxiously hoping the writers would remember everything correctly? No. It was Jesus who said that God's Spirit would ensure that the apostles would "*remember*" all that he had taught them.[67] Jesus commends the Bible not merely as written by men but as having complete integrity as the word of God. If you question the credibility of the Bible, you are questioning Jesus himself, because he has tied his reputation to it. Once again the foundation is the person and integrity of Jesus.

I know that in the past you have dismissed belief in the afterlife as being in the realm of the "unknowable". If you read from the top of my pyramid below, then it does seem outlandish to say such things as "we can know about the afterlife" or that "the Bible is inspired by God". However, there are foundational reasons underpinning these statements. In contrast, if you *read it from the bottom up*, you'll see that the upper decks are built on solid logical and historical grounds.

If you look closely at all the evidence we've discussed, then even the very existence of God can be tackled from a legal and historical perspective.

I initially treated the existence of "a God" tenderly, as in: "*If there is a God, has he communicated…?*" Most of us, when faced with the question, "Is there a God?", tend to look at the vast universe and stare into the infinite starry night and throw our

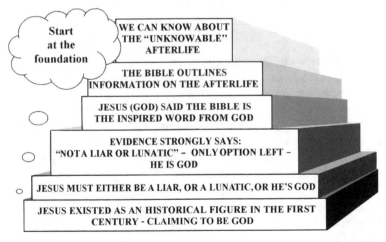

Start at the foundation

WE CAN KNOW ABOUT THE "UNKNOWABLE" AFTERLIFE

THE BIBLE OUTLINES INFORMATION ON THE AFTERLIFE

JESUS (GOD) SAID THE BIBLE IS THE INSPIRED WORD FROM GOD

EVIDENCE STRONGLY SAYS: "NOT A LIAR OR LUNATIC" – ONLY OPTION LEFT – HE IS GOD

JESUS MUST EITHER BE A LIAR, OR A LUNATIC, OR HE'S GOD

JESUS EXISTED AS AN HISTORICAL FIGURE IN THE FIRST CENTURY - CLAIMING TO BE GOD hands in the air and say, "How could you possibly know for sure?" "How can you test that?"

But if God has come into history, looking for God "out there" is like looking for your sunglasses all over your house when they were on top of your head all the time.

If the evidence says Christ was neither a liar nor a lunatic, then God has come into the world – right here among us. Because he made himself one of us, he is testable and tangible. History does not question the existence of Jesus Christ. The only question left is whether he was lying in his claim, or whether he *is* God. If we conclude that Christ was not lying, then he is God, and obviously God does exist!

Rita, I like your concept of "God is You"! (So would you mind doing something about all this rain?)

Oh, but haven't I determined what the concept of God should be? No, I haven't. Jesus Christ has. We can argue about our different *concepts* of God, but it's not me you'll be arguing with. Christ is the one who defined God as a personal being rather than an impersonal force. He is the one who said that the God of the Bible is the one true God, transcendent, rather than "God is in everyone". If you have a different concept of God then you must know more than Jesus Christ.

I saw a great sign from above – *drink Foster's lager*

Sorry if all of this is not what you have in mind when you think of evidence for God's existence. You didn't get your "sign" or "voice from the sky" as proof, but I don't think it would help anyway. In a year's time you'd be wondering whether the voice might not have been inside your head. Asylums are full of people who have "heard" from God. In contrast, the historical facts we have examined have remained unchanged for 2,000 years. The teaching of Jesus says there are two reasons why we have all the evidence we need:

1. Because of the awesome wonder and detail of the world, "the things that have been made", there is "no excuse" for *anyone* not believing in the existence of God.[68] Remember, it couldn't have popped out of nothing!
2. Jesus has provided all the evidence we need to believe that his claim about himself was true. According to Jesus' teaching, if you're not satisfied with what is written, then you wouldn't be convinced even if someone came back from the dead to tell you.[69] The problem is no longer an intellectual one.

If it's okay for you, it's croquet for me

It's so easy to say, "Well that's okay, but why do *I* need all this anyway?" – What is the need?

After all, if you are happy in your life, secure within yourself, happy in your own beliefs, you don't hurt anyone and you try to be nice to people, what does it matter whether it is true or not anyway?

"If it makes others happy, fine, but why do *I* need any of this?"

The answer is, you *don't* need any of this to make you happy or feel good: you already have that. In fact I'll go a step further and say you don't need any of this *at all*!

If…

If you can be certain at the bottom of your heart and mind that Jesus Christ was a liar or a lunatic.

The trouble is, if he wasn't, then according to his teaching there is a tremendously pressing need.

And what is that need?

I thought you'd never ask.

8

So what difference does it make anyway?

Finally, I want to address your question as to what difference all of this makes if it is true. What if Jesus is God and his teaching is true? How does this affect us? To address this we need to start with the essential teaching of Jesus, which is both justice and love.

The idea of justice seems attractive to us, but it is actually the bad news. After all, if God is perfectly just and brings "*every* deed into judgment, including *every* hidden thing",[70] that must include every deed and everyone! We're in trouble!

Most people love to point the finger at others, saying, "Well, no one is perfect, and I'm not as bad as some." They think this is a loophole, or a reason why they won't have to account for their own wrongdoing. But a God of perfect justice will not deal with only the worst offenders. That would not be justice even by our imperfect standards. For example, should a judge sentence a mass murderer to jail but let off a single murderer because, relatively speaking, he's not as bad as the other guy?

Where do you draw the line? Should murderers and child molesters receive justice? Of course! How about wife-bashers? Surely them too! How about the husbands who emotionally torment their wives? Them as well! And the selfishly cruel people in the world? Well, yes. And what about people who have cheated on their tax? Hey! Wait a minute! Leave me out of this. Just stick to the murderers.

You see, Rita, we draw the line at our own standard (wherever that is), not a perfect standard. The only way there could ever be true justice is if *every single deed* is taken into account.

I fought the law and the mother-in-law won

The bad news is that every one of us has done something wrong (don't I know it!). You don't have to be a believer to agree with the New Testament statement that:

> **If we claim to be without sin, we deceive ourselves and the truth is not in us.**[71]

Remember the Ten Commandments? (Not the movie.) Even many atheists have a sort of distant respect for them: "Yeah, I go along with the Ten Commandments – I never killed anybody." In fact, three out of the five major world religions believe in the Ten Commandments. The Jews, the Christians and even the Muslims at least pay lip-service to them, because the commandments are found in the first five books of the Bible (the Torah), which the Muslims also believe is God's word. The problem is not finding people who believe in the Ten Commandments; the problem is – have we obeyed them? In fact, when was the last time you even read them?

Well, let's have a look at them now (along with commentary from Jesus or other New Testament writers on each commandment). But no pulling a "Pharisee" on me. Jesus told a parable about a Pharisee, a "good" man, who condemned himself when he thought that his lawbreaking should be overlooked – just because he had not broken the law as many times as others.[72] It's called justifying yourself. It's human nature, isn't it? What is the first thing you say when the policeman pulls you over for speeding? "Well really officer, I'm normally a good driver... and ... and ... and if anything, you should be out looking for the real criminals – the bank robbers and the evildoers." And of course that line is always a winner with the policeman, who immediately responds with, "Well of course, why didn't I think of that? I'm going off to get me some bank robbers and evildoers! Whatever came over me disturbing a good citizen like you?"

Well, maybe in your dreams. If anything, the policeman would be doubly insulted because you're asking him to be corrupt and overlook your lawbreaking, on the basis that there are others who have broken the law more severely than you have. It doesn't work that way with law enforcers either above or below. In fact, the New Testament says that if you stumble at even one point of the law then you are a "whole" lawbreaker.[73] In other words, as we look at the commandments, just remember the rule of thumb: if you do the crime, you do the time!

THE TEN COMMANDMENTS

1. **You shall have no other gods before me...**
   Love the Lord your God with all your heart and with all your soul and with all your mind and with all your strength.
   (Mark 12:30)

81

2. *You shall not make for yourself an idol in the form of anything in heaven above or on the earth beneath or in the waters below…*
   They worshipped and served created things rather than the Creator… (Romans 1:25)

3. *You shall not misuse the name of the Lord your God…*
   But I tell you that men will have to give account on the day of judgment for every careless word they have spoken. (Matthew 12:36)

4. *Remember the Sabbath day by keeping it holy. Six days you shall labour and do all your work but the seventh day is a Sabbath to the Lord your God…*
   You should not stay away from the church meetings, as some are doing. (Hebrews 10:25, NCV)

5. *Honour your father and your mother…*
   Children, obey your parents in the Lord, for this is right. (Ephesians 6:1)

6. *You shall not murder…*
   You have heard it said, "…anyone who murders will be subject to judgment". But I tell you that anyone who is angry with his brother will be subject to judgment.
   (Matthew 5:21–22)

7. **You shall not commit adultery...**
   But I tell you that anyone who looks at a woman lustfully has already committed adultery with her in his heart.
   (Matthew 5:28)

8. **You shall not steal...**
   Do not be deceived: ...thieves...will not inherit the kingdom of God.   (1 Corinthians 6:9–10)

9. **You shall not give false testimony [lie]...**
   ...and all liars – their place will be in the fiery lake of burning sulphur.   (Revelation 21:8)

10. **You shall not covet...anything that belongs to your neighbour [improperly desire what is not yours]...**
    ...you...covet, but cannot have what you want. (James 4:2)

    ...I am he who searches hearts and minds, and I will repay each of you according to your deeds.

                                                              (Revelation 2:23)

Assault and batteries not included

One of the areas where our society seems to have agreement with the Bible is in the concept that good deeds cannot erase bad deeds. For instance, take a look at my next illustration. We don't expect the judge to let off the bank robber, no matter how many good deeds he has done. That would be ludicrous. This is why I say that society is in complete agreement with the Bible on this one, and yet for some reason we think it's going to be different in God's dealings with us. It seems that we think the idea of good deeds excusing bad deeds is illogical, unless it involves us! We look at those commandments and start justifying ourselves with the times we think we have kept the law – as if that would somehow make our lawbreaking disappear. It doesn't work that way in everyday life, let alone with a perfect judge who brings "every deed into judgment, including every hidden thing".[74]

I put this concept to the test years ago. Before I reformed my driving habits I managed to get my photo taken going through a red light at one of those traffic intersections where they have automatic red-light cameras. It was not a very good shot. I wasn't smiling at the time. You receive a fine in the mail and you can send for the photographic evidence that confirms that it was really you driving through the red light. That's when you send off your cheque to pay the fine. But I wanted to test to see if good deeds can outweigh bad deeds. So, rather than send back the cheque with the fine, I sent them back another photo.

I ADMIT I ROBBED THE BANK, YOUR HONOUR... BUT I'VE BEEN IN LOTS OF BANKS I HAVEN'T ROBBED... EVEN PUT SOME MONEY INTO A FEW OF THEM... AND I HELP LITTLE OLD LADIES ACROSS THE STREET... WHETHER THEY WANNA GO OR NOT...

One of me driving through a green light!

I even gave them lots of different photos of me driving through lots of different green lights. Hey, that should convince them that I'm a good driver, right? But I still had to pay the fine. I didn't get off. If you think that's a bit loony (and it is), it's no different from when we try to excuse ourselves if we break God's law. According to standards of true justice, no amount of good things we do can erase a wrong deed we've committed. Our good deeds can't balance out bad deeds because good deeds don't *exceed* what is right: they only *meet* what is right. You say, "Doesn't trying to be a good person count for something? I don't hurt anyone; I try to be nice to people?" And the answer is... So what, shouldn't you always? Being nice to people is the *least* we should do; it is not *more* than what we should do. It doesn't "store up any points" to offset against bad deeds.

The good, the bad and the medley

So what will a perfectly just God do with us? Clearly he must punish *every single* wrong deed. Each and every person is deserving of punishment for his or her wrongdoings. We all deserve justice! Here is where the holiness and justice of a perfect God cannot be fully comprehended by self-serving man:

God is light; in him there is no darkness at all.[75]

Because God is truly holy and just, the smallest wrongdoing is darkness, which separates us from God and puts him off as much as the vilest murderer puts us off.

As far as a perfect God is concerned, a wrong act we do is not something that, once committed, is "in the past". For an eternal

85

God (existing outside time), everything that happens – past, present and future – exists *now!* A wrong act is not forgotten or cancelled in time by good deeds. It continues to exist and must be dealt with.

If the sum total of our life's good works were an 8-ounce glass of fresh pure milk, then a wrong deed would be a drop of cyanide. If you mixed them together, would you drink it just because you could confidently say there are still 8 ounces of actual milk in the glass? After all, it has the appearance of being a pure glass of milk. Would you weigh it out and say, "Hey, at least there are still 8 ounces of good milk in there."? No way, chum! As long as you're aware of what's in that glass you couldn't care less even if the good milk outweighed the cyanide a million to one. You would not touch that milk. Not unless every drop of that cyanide were removed *and accounted for! Every single drop!*

A God who is perfect cannot allow our wrongdoing to go unaccounted for, either. He will deal with the smallest impurity. It's not just a case of his wanting to punish wrong deeds. If he is perfectly holy and just, he *must* punish them!

Till death do us part-time

I'm personally sceptical of the value of subjective experiences such as *Near-Death Experiences* (if you're dead how can you be *nearly* dead?), but it makes for an interesting parallel.

Those who have had N.D.E.s speak of a brilliant beautiful light. Among other things, the Bible describes God as pure holy light. It also says that for any darkness that approaches him, he is a consuming fire[76] (pure light burning up that which is dark). We can all enjoy the beauty and warm light of the sun, but if you could actually get close enough, the sun would burn you to a frazzle. Perhaps all these N.D.E. people who see the beautiful light at the end of the long tunnel, but always manage to turn back, should be thankful that they never got too close.

We think the big problem is, why does God allow suffering and evil? (I will deal with this later.) But the real big problem is, what if God *does* do something about suffering and evil? What if God is not *less* concerned about bad deeds than we are, but is much *more* concerned than we are?

He might choose to delay the justice but he won't ignore it. It's like the policeman who follows behind you in an unmarked police car while you're speeding along the motorway. He might stay there for a while before he decides to pull you over. In that time you are unaware and unworried and, besides, there are so many other drivers speeding faster than you, so it can't be that bad. In fact you might even be annoyed by some of those real menaces on the road who are driving so much more erratically than you. And yet the policeman is behind *you* all this time, letting you fully soak in your choice to break the law. He doesn't just let you go speeding indefinitely. He chooses a time when he thinks enough is enough, and then says, "Pull over, driver." All that good time you thought you were making suddenly grinds to a halt. It turns out your actions were being recorded all along, and now you have to pay the price.

With God, the policeman is behind everyone else as well.

Believe me, it's not easy being perfict

Contrary to popular opinion, there are things that a perfect God cannot do, otherwise he would no longer be perfect. He *cannot* lie. He *cannot* pervert his holiness. He *cannot* be unjust. God cannot do anything that would make him less – less than a perfect God. When he says that the wages of sin are death and judgment, according to the things we have done,[77] that is simply a factual statement of perfect justice (from a perspective that you and I don't have). It is not arbitrary, as if he could have made it, "the wages of sin are 20 spoonfuls of castor oil". If it were the least bit more or less exacting than "death and judgment according to the things we've done", then it would not be perfect.

This perfect justice of God is the *bad* news as far as we're concerned. In fact all the major world religions seem to agree on what the problem is. They all say that if you have done something wrong, then justice must be done. There is a price to pay. But that is no help to us. So what if everyone agrees on the problem – what about a solution? If justice is all there is on offer, then we are in big trouble! In fact, the justice required for the times we have broken the commandments of an *eternal* God must mean an *eternal* penalty. Remember, an eternal God sees transgressions eternally, so he must deal with them eternally. He can't change his mind about justice after a few years or so.

Now it's only fair that we pay for our own lawbreaking. It wouldn't be fair if someone else did. And even if someone wanted to, it would have to be someone who had never ever sinned. After all, I can't offer to do time in jail for you if I'm already in jail under my own sentence. And even if someone were perfect and were willing to take our place, they would have to be willing to receive an eternal punishment. Otherwise the books of justice wouldn't add up.

That is, unless this someone was eternal *themselves*, and took on death and punishment. But wait a minute? How could there ever be such a substitute? Who could ever take on that much punishment? And who has never ever sinned except God? And who is eternal except God? And how does anyone who is eternal die?

I can't get no sanctification

God in the person of the eternal Son, Jesus, came into this world and lived as one of us. A human being who never sinned. When he went to the cross, it wasn't to die a death such as we imagine.

Jesus was fully conscious of his eternal relationship with God the Father. Although Jesus was truly a man, he was also truly God (and here is where I admit this is beyond trying to fathom), but something *eternal* went on at that cross. A separation took place that is wider than time itself. Jesus cried, "My God, My God, why have you forsaken me?"[78] Jesus experienced all of the pain and judgment that our sin deserves, including being *forsaken* by God.

While God is more concerned than we are about justice and judgment on the one hand, he is also more concerned than we are about love and mercy on the other. This is the "good news" (the word "gospel" means "good news"). It was God the Father who gave up his own Son to take on the hell we deserve, and the Son went willingly. It was none less than God who humbled himself to become a man to take our place in punishment:

...Christ Jesus: Who, being in very nature God...made himself nothing...being made in human likeness...he humbled himself and became obedient to death – even death on a cross! [79]

Because he is God eternal (not limited in time), Jesus' death becomes the substitute judgment for many people in all times. Hence the Old Testament faithful believers looked forward in hope to the coming Messiah (which means Christ). They also received the benefits of Jesus' work on the cross.

God's love gives us freedom from judgment as a free gift to us, while the price demanded by his perfect justice has been paid in full. True forgiveness is not cheap. Out of love you might forgive your little son for acting like "Prambo", breaking your window, but someone still has to pay for the window. If you have a cheap view of the demands of justice, you will have a cheap view of the love of God who paid such a great price for our forgiveness.

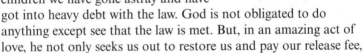

This parent/child example is a relevant analogy. We are not naturally children of God; we are naturally creatures of God. God the Father has only one natural Son, his co-eternal Son, Jesus. And yet like wayward children we have gone astray and have got into heavy debt with the law. God is not obligated to do anything except see that the law is met. But, in an amazing act of love, he not only seeks us out to restore us and pay our release fee,

90

he adopts us as his very own children. The trouble is that, like most children, we just don't want to swallow our pride and admit our need of that adoption. We would rather take our own chances with the law. Because of this we are all responsible for the fact that one day we will all meet God as either our Father or our judge.

The Bible says that breaking God's law is sin. That is the Bible's definition of sin. It is not something some "Church man" made up. By having faith in Jesus, we will be "saved". Saved from what? From judgment for all the wrong things we have ever done, thought or said. All those things will be transferred to the cross of Christ. As Jesus himself says:

> *Very truly I tell you, anyone who hears my word and believes him who sent me has eternal life and does not come under judgment but has passed from death to life.*[80]

Stand up on your seat, I don't want this to go over your head!

Let's just pause a moment to try to take this on board. Human beings cannot fully appreciate the love of Christ in dying for us because, in the first place, we can't comprehend how much our sin grieves God. Have you ever noticed the difference in attitude between the person who does something wrong and the person who has been wronged? Think about it in our relationships. One person is hurt and the other can be almost oblivious to what the other is feeling. If you ask the bank robber whether he thinks the bank teller is his enemy, he will tell you, "No, it is nothing personal; I just want the money." But then ask the bank teller with a gun shoved in his face if that robber is an enemy. Of course! It's all a matter of perspective. Sin is the greatest antithesis of the character of God. He is totally opposed to all sin, down to the smallest detail. In the perspective of a perfect God, our wrong deeds make us his "enemies". Jesus dying for us is not like dying for someone who is good. It's more like a person murdering your son, and while the murderer is on death row you offer to take the *murderer's* place on the gallows. As the New Testament says:

> *... when we were God's enemies, we were reconciled to him through the death of his Son.*[81]

Until we see how much we have offended God, we can't see how great is his love. As long as we see ourselves by our own standard, as "good people", we can't tap into the magnitude of this love and what it means to have God give up everything for us:

> *Very rarely will anyone die for a righteous man, though for a good man someone might possibly dare to die. But God demonstrates his own love for us in this: While we were still sinners, Christ died for us.*[82]

Religion: it ain't what you know, it's *who* you know

God does not ask us first to reach a certain standard of goodness or wait until our lives are "together" before we can receive this gift.

The gift depends on what *he* has done, not on what we can do. We can receive the forgiveness *he* paid for, simply by accepting it as we are now:

> *It is by grace [an undeserved gift] you have been saved, ...not by works, so that no one can boast."*[83]

When Christians claim to be going to heaven, they are not boasting in themselves, but in Christ's ability to pay their debt.

So Christians are not "good people", deserving of going to heaven, at all. It's a mistake to object that you're as good a person as any Christian. Christians are not making any claims about themselves. Their substitute at judgment is Jesus Christ. It's their substitute with whom you have to compare yourself, if you want to say that you're good enough for heaven. God's standard for heaven is perfect obedience to the law. No one imperfect can ever enter heaven.[84] Christ is God's entrance standard for heaven and, because he offers himself as a substitute, that standard is available to everyone – who will believe:

> *If you confess with your mouth, "Jesus is Lord," and believe in your heart that God raised him from the dead, you will be saved.*[85]

Just believe. Nothing more. But nothing less! To believe "*Jesus is Lord*", and to believe what he did with his life, death and resurrection. To really believe that it is your sin that he was punished for is to have a whole new attitude towards all that he tells us is sin as laid out in his word (as opposed to my own definition of "sin").

To believe he was raised to life for my new life is to be in a new relationship with him as Lord. To believe in him as Lord is to believe what he said. The first words he said at the beginning of his ministry were, "*Repent, for the kingdom of heaven is near*".[86] The word "repentance" comes from the Greek word *metanoia*. It means a turning or changing of mind and heart. This is a genuine confession and sorrow for having grieved him. To believe that he literally went through that pain on the cross for you. (And here is the key – everything else adds up to nothing if you miss this!) True repentance is to have an ongoing change of heart towards deliberately sinning.

How do you know all of what sinning is? We already saw it laid out in the Ten Commandments. If you want more detail, look it up! Start by reading the New Testament and get Jesus' definition. Repentance does not mean becoming perfect. If we could become perfect he wouldn't have had to die on the cross in our place. But if you *believe* he took an eternity worth of hell on that cross for your personal sin, then you will desire to make every effort not to sin against that cross and the relationship that God secured at such a great price. No one who is in a relationship of love can go on *deliberately* hurting the other if that love is genuine. To ignore repentance is not true belief, it is hypocrisy.

Christianity is a bit like an amnesty. An example of amnesty occurred in Australia when the government declared semi-automatic guns illegal. The government provided an amnesty and bought back all the illegal guns. Here's a case where *you* are the one in possession of something that is illegal, yet the government not only pardons you, but also pays the full price for you to get rid of it. But there are two conditions to amnesty:

1. To receive the free pardon and payment, you have to come forward and hand over that which is illegal. In this case, you had to hand over your illegal guns.
2. There is a time limit. With the guns it was one year. If you get caught with illegal guns after that year, no pardon, no payment – *you* pay!

The time limit for our amnesty is this lifetime. We don't know when our time limit is going to run out. But if this free gift of amnesty is so good, then why isn't everyone falling over to grab hold of it? In fact, why would Jesus say that there will be "many" who say they believe and even call him "Lord", but will be in for a big shock on the day of judgment when he says, "away from me, you evildoers, I never knew you"?[87] Why wouldn't everyone want to get in on this?

Well, the main reason is not because of the evidence (I haven't met anyone yet who looked honestly at the evidence and concluded that Jesus was a liar), and it's not because the gift is not great enough. God giving up his only Son? He could not have done more. No, the reason why most people will ultimately reject this free gift of Christ is simply this –

Most people don't want to give up their guns!

I heard church is for hypocrites
(so I thought I'd better start going)

I hope this answers your question as to why I now attend a church on Sundays.

Not because it will get me to heaven. I've already been given that for free.

Not to make me a good or more worthy person (recognizing I'm not good is the first step towards turning to God in faith and repentance).

Not to make me feel better (I already felt fine).

Only for the simple reason that to be honest with the consequence of believing Jesus told the truth, I have no option but to "believe" in him as Lord of my life. I therefore do what he says. As the New Testament says, anyone who says he is Christian...

> ***...but does not do what he commands is a liar, and the truth is not in him.***[88]

Real hypocrisy would be for me to call him Lord, and *not* "do what he commands".

Distinctive and not so distinctive Marx

Perhaps the greatest contrast between the teaching in the New Testament and every other religion and philosophy in the world's history is this: in all others, man is trying to find answers from his own goodness, to reach God or a level of spirituality, or even to

96

attain the right political ideology – Karl Marx, for instance. Man is trying to be good enough to get to heaven or reach Nirvana, etc. But the teaching of Christ is – God reaching out to man (reaching the standard for us) and seeking us.

The most fascinating objection to Christianity is the complaint that "Christians think theirs is the only way". I say it's fascinating because, in the big picture, Jesus is the only one who ever *offered* a way. Remember, the common denominator of the world religions is that they all agree on the problem. There is a price to pay for wrongdoing. All the religions are therefore trying to help us to stop making the problem get worse. Do this and don't do that, and the problem will not become greater. But what if you have already done wrong? And what if you do wrong again? The Buddha in the Dhammapada (teachings of the Buddha) said that the answer is that each one must pay the price individually:

"By oneself the evil is done, by oneself one suffers; by oneself evil is left undone, by oneself one is purified. The pure and impure (stand and fall) by themselves, no one can purify another.[89]

No one can purify another! In other words, if the deed is done, then you must pay and there is no other way. Jesus offered to do what others didn't even conceive of. He offered a way. In fact he said, "I am the way, the truth and the life." What way? He offered his life as a ransom. A way for us to have the price of our sin paid in full.

Bad people go to heaven

Bad people go to heaven? Sounds crazy? But this is the point we've been making and I want to make sure you don't miss it. The New Testament actually teaches that *bad* people go to heaven and *good* people go to hell. At least the ones who trust in their own goodness. You've heard this one before:

"I'm a reasonably good person. I've done a few things wrong but I'm not as bad as some, so if there is anything afterwards I'll be alright." Does this sound familiar?

The person who says this has their faith in their own "goodness". They are the true "boasters", effectively saying, "If there's a heaven then *I'm good enough* to get there." In contrast, Christianity is about faith in the goodness of Christ rather than boasting in your own "goodness".

Jesus has a sobering message for those who rely on their own goodness "compared to others". He gave the example of two men: one ended up in heaven and the other one ended up in hell. (Check the footnote* if you want to see whether it was the "good" man or the "bad" man who made it.)

The New Testament teaches that only bad people go to heaven, that is, people who acknowledge their "badness" and humbly turn

---

* *"Two men went up to the temple to pray, one a Pharisee and the other a tax collector. The Pharisee stood up and prayed about himself: 'God, I thank you that I am not like other men – robbers, evildoers, adulterers – or even like this tax collector, I fast twice a week and give a tenth of all I get.' But the tax collector stood at a distance. He would not even look up to heaven, but beat his breast and said, 'God, have mercy on me, a sinner.' I tell you that this man rather than the other, went home justified before God."* (Luke 18:10–14)

to God. Submitting to him as the Lord of their life, and their Saviour from judgment.

Once upon a time-bomb

Though the Bible was written over a period of 1,500 years by 40 authors and comprises 66 books, it is remarkably consistent in its theme of God's redemption of man.

The Bible teaches us that this life is but a spit of time. A time that can run out very quickly. The true meaning of our short space of time here is the decision we make that determines where we will spend eternity.

I could believe in fate, if it wasn't so fatal

I think the New Testament is straightforward enough for anyone to read for themselves and see its essential message. However, I don't think anyone could possibly take it all in at a single sitting. I read it eight times before I noticed the significance of Acts 17:26–27. If you believe in fate or destiny then you might pick up the significance of these words much more quickly than I did:

From one man he made every nation of men, that they should inhabit the whole earth; and he determined the times set for them and the exact places where they should live.

That means our exact times and places are not mere coincidence. There is a purpose or "fate" in everything – the people who cross our paths (our exact time and place) and the things that happen to us, even the bad things. But what is this purpose? The very next line tells us:

> **God did this so that men would seek him and perhaps reach out for him…though he is not far from each one of us.**

It wasn't "fate" orchestrating our "exact time and place": it was God all along. The true meaning of our "spit of time" in this life is to determine where we end up in eternity. Circumstances of our life, even the bad things, are for one major purpose: to give us a jolt into taking a closer look at life and therefore a greater opportunity to seek and find God (although not all will grab that opportunity).

Society's way of looking at things says that when bad things happen to you, causing physical or emotional hardship, then you are on the "bottom rung". But think about it. When do most people start to ask questions about God? It's usually when major things happen or at some low point. Those who are jolted by adversity into really thinking about crucial issues of life are sometimes better off than the "happy" people who have everything and "don't need religion".

Excuse me, waiter! (Let me give you a tip)

But why wait until you're at some low or vulnerable point before investigating? Doesn't it make more sense to go for it while your thinking is at its most rational and critical?

It's a sad indication of our self-serving nature that for the "happy secure person who doesn't need religion" it often takes apparent ill fortune for them even to think about the one who gave us life. At least in this respect it seems apparent that ill fortune can be advantageous in the greater perspective. Which is probably why Jesus said:

> **Blessed are the poor in spirit, for theirs is the kingdom of heaven.**[90]

Well, Rita, if you've got this far, thanks for staying with me and letting me share all this with you. At least perhaps you can see more of the importance of these issues and realize why I've gone to the trouble of writing the "world's longest letter". I don't believe a person can or should make up someone else's mind for them on these issues. I just hope that you don't dismiss the New Testament without reading it for yourself. It could matter. For ever.

> With love,
> from your brother-in-law,
> Bill

P.S. Please don't take out my Appendix (i)

My investigation led me to centre most questions on Christ and the Bible because the evidence challenged me to, but there is another reason for this focus. Most of your questions attempt to challenge the God of the Bible, rather than other religions. Like most people, you didn't think to put the other religions to the same stringent testing.

Would you ever think to ask a Hindu tricky questions like, "Why does God allow suffering?" When was the last time anyone questioned the accuracy of Buddha's teachings because they weren't written down until centuries after his death? It's the God of the Bible people question, and this is the case with your remaining questions.

Important as they are, I'm looking at these appendices as afterthoughts. Why? Because up to now we have been hard-headed searchers after evidence. None of these following questions throws doubt on the actual evidence. Emotional issues such as "why is there suffering in the world?" and "how can God be a jealous God?", are questions about the *nature* of God, not the *existence* of God or whether he has communicated to man. Nevertheless, these points can be satisfactorily explained in a way consistent with a good God.

Once this internal consistency is established, still to "disagree" because you think things "should be" different, or because you don't "like" them, is to let go of our quest to use logic. If we didn't make it to point C, it should have been on the basis of evidence, not of details we "dislike" about the God of the Bible or our disagreement on emotional views. If we *have* been able to get to point C, then disagreeing with God on how things are run is like you confidently taking a flying leap off the top of the Rialto building because you've decided you now "disagree" with the law of gravity. Facts are not dependent on whether you "like" them or not.

Before I started my investigation, I thought that if there was a greater being who has communicated with man, then this greater being would have to be on a totally superior level of intellect to myself. For example, a computer can never be of greater intelligence than the program it is given.

So if this "greater being" has communicated facts conflicting with my own views on the way *I* think things should be, does this mean I'm right and God is wrong? If God doesn't fit our preconception of what God "should be", do we then conclude that he can't be the real God?

If God is jealous, I wouldn't mess with him

You mentioned that God shouldn't have mere human emotions such as anger or jealousy. Firstly, this is merely your personal opinion of what God "should be" (as if we were creating God in our image rather than the other way around), but what if these were God's emotions before they were ours? If God is perfect then his emotions would not be flawed in our self-serving way. Rather, they just might be greater and pure versions of our emotions. For example, the Hebrew dictionary tells us:

> El qanna: Jealous; used in our language in an evil sense, has a somewhat different meaning in the Hebrew in the Old Testament... God asserts his claim [to what is rightfully his].[91]

Jealousy here is a fierce loyalty to what is good and right and just.

God's jealousy for righteousness and justice is not a mere preference or whim, but the standard on which a perfect God *must* insist. But a perfect God who is the source of all perfection can have no higher standard than himself. He does not need anything from us. He has everything already. But if we give honour that is due to him to anyone or anything else, then that would be falsehood, and God cannot condone falsehood.

Appendix (ii)

If there's so much evidence, why don't more people believe?

Since when is truth measured by weight of numbers? If it were, I suppose Christianity might still have a case, since it is by far the largest religion in the world (33.7%).[92] One in every three people in the world professes the Christian faith (I am not suggesting everyone who professes faith is a true follower, but that goes for all beliefs). But if the evidence is so strong, why don't even more people believe?

To answer this it may be helpful to examine at least one major misconception about what belief or faith means. And it's ironic that it is the Western world, with its "I know, I know, I know…" attitude, that seems to hold more misconceptions about the Christian faith than many other parts of the world that don't assume they already "know it all". I wonder why Western people think Christianity is a Western religion, when its origin and the largest percentage of its practice today is not in the West at all.

Of myth and men

It seems the non-Christian West makes up its own definition, that faith in the Bible is a "belief in the existence of God" or "belief in the unbelievable". The Bible, however, agrees far more with the Oxford Dictionary, which defines faith as "trust or reliance on an authority". Now we're getting somewhere! Do we know anyone who would cringe at the thought of submitting to an authority other than themselves, no matter how convincing the evidence is?

Many people know the Bible teaches that those who have faith or belief in Jesus will be "forgiven for their sins" or "saved". Many seem to think that "belief" here means believing in the mere existence of Jesus. If that's all it means, then every serious historian must be Christian! Jesus certainly told his apostles they must believe in him. However, he can hardly have been referring to their belief in his existence, since he was right there "doing a live appearance" when he told them this.

The Bible actually laughs at the idea that mere belief in God's existence could "save" someone. The New Testament records an early example of sarcastic wit when Jesus' own brother James asks, "So you believe there is one God?" and then answers himself, saying, "Good! Even the demons believe that – and shudder." [93]

– "Is there anyone out there?"
– "YES, I AM HERE, YOUR LORD AND JUDGE."
– "...Is there anyone else out there?"

The apostle John records that there were some Jewish leaders who:

...believed in him but...would not confess their faith...for they loved praise from men more than praise from God. [94]

106

These Jewish leaders had all the evidence they needed to believe in Jesus. They had seen and heard him; they believed he was who he said he was, yet still had no faith. That is, they had no "trust or reliance on [his] authority" over them. In short, they would not permit their belief in him to direct their life, which is not a true belief at all.

No matter how convincing the evidence is, there will always be many who will not allow belief to enter their life. Even if Jesus were on earth today, many convinced people would stop short of confessing faith in him. Why? Because there is something else that competes with facts and evidence and, in the end, impresses us more – our pride.

Pride makes it difficult for us to accept the authority of anything outside ourselves, even the "authority" of sound evidence. Of course it is important, as we have been saying, to test the soundness of evidence. But pride's battle against the claims of Jesus Christ goes on long after the strength of the evidence is established.

For some people, even the thought of being labelled a "Christian" makes evidence a secondary consideration. Others refuse to look openly at the evidence because they associate Christianity with hypocrites, those who fight wars over religion, priests who have molested children, and so on. But this is the mentality of those who join religious cults. The cult member makes a human leader the "god" they believe in (or God's representative), and these critics are making "religious people" the "god" they *reject*. In both cases, Jesus is assessed on the basis of other human beings. And once again the critic finds an excuse to ignore the actual evidence.

The behaviour of some "religious" people is a weak excuse for not investigating the *actual teaching* for ourselves. Until we do, Jesus Christ, the one who spent most of his ministry in dispute with the pious "religious people" of his day, doesn't get an honest hearing.

Blowing out your "brains" theory

I think you can have brains and faith too. I don't think everyone needs to sift through the mountains of evidence that I have, to become a believer. The fact that not all Christians have a great evidential defence for their faith shows that God doesn't discriminate according to knowledge:

> *Blessed are those who have not seen [all the evidence?] and yet have believed.*[95]

Nevertheless, I think you'd be surprised how many brilliant intellectual Christians there are in all fields of study. Just don't expect to see them pop up on "Meet the Press". As Tony Campolo, a Christian sociologist, once pointed out, the difference between the notorious tele-evangelists and all the rest of us is that you've never heard of the rest of us. In my opinion you never will, either. There is no media mileage in intelligent pro-Christianity.

Close encounters of the "foot" kind

Having examined the religious sources at first hand, I have come to a point where I really think that Christianity is based on sound historical and tangible evidence. Faith or belief (as the Bible describes it) is the response to the evidence, not the blind acceptance of it. It is certainly not just a "feeling" or "belief in the unbelievable".

I find it an incredible irony that it's those who want to dismiss New Testament faith as unreasonable, who revert to denying tangibles and logic when confronted with imponderable evidence. "But it can't be. Just believing that Jesus told the truth. It can't be that simple," you say. (Before, you were complaining that there was no evidence, and now it's *too* simple!) I've even heard people say, "But there must be something else to it…even if it's all true, how do we know if we're really even *here*?"

To the person who asks this, I would suggest they allow me a 50-metre run-up to deliver them a kick in the pants – just to test if they're really here or not! I think it was C.S. Lewis who said there are some things that shouldn't have to be explained; whether it concerns God or not: nonsense will always remain nonsense. Who would have thought when we started out that religion would be appealing to rationality, while the arguments against it let go of rational thought?

With sincere apologies to genuine existentialists (who unfortunately could never be sure if my apology really existed), I've never met anyone yet who really lives their life as if they "aren't really here". At least, not when it comes down to the "self" needs. These kinds of arguments are often only selectively brought up as an excuse to deny uncomfortable facts. Here is the use of logic and rational argument to deny logic and rationality. This is what happens when the rational bloke investigating religion finds evidence that he really didn't expect or want to find. He suddenly becomes so open-minded as to let his brains fall out, and suddenly begins to question things like whether or not he's "really here".

Mr Spock – the final front ear

Another "last-resort" attempt to escape the "God" factor is the idea that life originated from superior beings from outer space. This is known as "panspermia". If you think it through, you'll soon realize that even Captain Kirk would be disappointed with this one. It doesn't solve any problems. After all, this doesn't explain the origin of life. (Where did these happy fliers come from in the first place?) In fact we still have two other problems:

1. We still have a "superior being" (or God) as our creator.
2. We still haven't got away from having to explain away Jesus as a monstrous liar. Panspermia might sound like a new alternative, but it's really just shifting the same old problems to a new planet.

"If you can't see it, it doesn't exist" (are we still talking about your brains?)

Irrational denials (along with unreasoning acceptance) of evidence contrast with the thinking in the New Testament, which warns its readers to use their brains, to check the evidence against facts. It warns them to:

"*Test everything*" [96] and to:

> *...see to it no one takes you captive through hollow and deceptive philosophy, which depends on human tradition.*[97]

It warns its readers to be careful of those who:

> *...to suit their own desires, will gather around them a great number of teachers to say what their itching ears want to hear... But you, keep your head in all situations...*[98]

The New Testament urges believers to be rational:

> *Always be prepared to give an answer to everyone who asks you to give the reason for the hope that you have.*[99]

The Greek word rendered "answer" is *apologia*. It is used elsewhere in the New Testament in the sense of an attorney giving a legal defence, not just any old "answer".

Even the greatest commandment of all (according to Jesus) is to:

> *Love the Lord your God with all your heart and with all your soul and with all your* mind.[100]

So if there's so much evidence, why don't more people believe? Simply because the evidence is not really the major issue. Check your own thinking. Have you had thoughts that cut across your appreciation of the evidence? For example, have you ever looked at a Christian and thought, "I would never want to end up like one of those people", or have you ever thought to yourself, "What would I have to give up if I became a believer?" If you have, then "consequences" have clouded objective and rational thinking.

We really have to stop pretending that we are not already extremely biased. Think about it this way. If all the difficult questions you ever had were answered to your full satisfaction, would you then be eager to give up those sins that displease God? Would you really want to testify that you are a Bible-believing Christian? If the answer is anything less than an enthusiastic "Yes!", then a bias has just been exposed. I'm not denying our right to genuine questions and concerns. But underlying them is an even deeper concern. We don't want to have to change our lives. None of us wants to give up our guns!

Appendix (iii)

The Bible is all a matter of interpretations

Before I read the Bible myself, this seemed like a fair criticism.
However, after reading it, I think it's more of an excuse we use –
"Hey, if all these Christians disagree with each other, then if there
is a God, he can't blame me if I give the whole thing a miss."

Rita, show me someone who says the Bible is all a matter of
interpretations and I'll show you someone who has:

1. Never read even the New Testament through once, and
2. Doesn't even know what the churches disagree over.

For instance, the most well-known division among professing
Christians is between Catholic and Protestant. The major
difference comes from the fact that one is directed by the Bible, and
the other is directed by both the Bible and church traditions.

Let's use a small issue as an example. One distinctively Catholic
doctrine is the "ascension of Mary"[101] (her bodily ascension into
heaven shortly after her death, which was declared officially in
1950). The outsider might imagine the Catholics and Protestants
sitting down over the Bible to debate an issue such as this, but
neither side is trying to say that the "ascension" is in the Bible (or
that all other Catholic declarations are necessarily in the Bible). At

113

this point I'm not concerned as to who is right or wrong. I'm simply making the point that the Bible is not what is in dispute with most individual doctrinal differences. It is a question of differences over just where authority is located. The Bible alone, or Bible "plus" traditions.

I've run into a few Presbyterians crossing

The average person's ignorance that Bible-believing denominations see themselves as different religions is also quite mistaken. Churches such as Assemblies of God, Baptist, Church of Christ, Presbyterian, Wesleyan (and the list goes on) have welcomed me not just to get another person through the door, but as a visiting Christian brother.

I've come across Presbyterian ministers guest-preaching at Baptist churches, and vice versa. This is not an uncommon thing between Bible-believing churches. It is not a superficial "tolerance" thing, but a genuine belief that there is no essential difference in their faith or religion.

The Bible-believing denominations agree on all major doctrines of the Bible, especially those concerning salvation. They also agree that none of them has authority to "interpret" or "add to" the Bible. The idea that these churches, with their authority only in the Bible, "interpret" essential doctrines of Christianity differently is a total fallacy, propped up largely by people who want an excuse to throw their hands in the air and say, "Well, who can you believe?"

Denominational divisions in the Christian church will be a fact of life wherever freedom of thought is allowed. Their existence reflects debate over non-essential areas that the Bible calls "disputable matters". In contrast, cult religions with as many as 5–10 million followers do not suffer this amount of division (denominations), because no individual thinking is allowed.

Let's look at an example. One matter that has been regarded as disputable (and yet still important) by Christians is baptism. Some denominations say sprinkle; some say dunk; some say do it as infants; some say do it only after you believe. Inevitably, as human beings, there will be differing opinions about disputable matters, but each person must be free to follow their own conscience. Bible churches have preferred to establish denominations that agree on all but these smaller disputable areas, rather than have one big church that has disagreement over secondary issues.

I object! Your odour!

It is acknowledged that these superficial divisions do occur over different interpretations of smaller points. Does this place a question mark over the Bible itself? Consider a parallel.

Two lawyers in a murder trial might argue the finer points of first- and second-degree murder. They are involved in a legitimate debate about interpretation of a law. Does this mean we should throw out the law against murder, saying, "The law stinks; it's all a matter of interpretation"?

The basics of the New Testament are straightforward and generally agreed upon. But the New Testament is not a kiddies' novel. I look back at the first time I read it and realize how little of it I understood, and yet in that first reading I still picked up three or four major points without consulting anyone. I later found out that these major points are those that *all* Bible-believing denominations agree upon as the *basic essentials* of Christianity and its doctrines.

Everything you always wanted to know about sects

So where do all these cults and "new interpretations" come from? Sects occur when people claim to have "special knowledge" (divine or otherwise), apart from the Bible. Cult leaders are the obvious example. But theologians with radical "new theories", such as the *Jesus Seminar* scholars, also fall into this category. This particular group of scholars managed to reduce the "only authentic" words of Jesus in the Lord's Prayer down to "Our Father". And what "scholarly" method do they use to achieve this? They gather together in seminars and have the words of Jesus printed overhead and then proceed to vote by holding up coloured slips of paper on whether they "think Jesus really would have said that". For instance, there was a great oral tradition in the first century. So if there are any long sentences, then the verdict is basically, "Nah, Jesus wouldn't have said that, chuck it out." And that portion of the text will get the "pink slip" (or black slip, or whatever).

The same group of scholars also elevate *The Gospel According to Thomas* to equal status with the New Testament gospels. With the exception of these *Jesus Seminar* theologians, scholars have generally agreed that the evidence is overwhelming that "*Thomas*" was written by Gnostics, a sect that didn't exist until about one hundred years after the New Testament gospels were written. Therefore, "*Thomas*" contributes about as much to the historical study of Jesus as his Tank Engine namesake. But it gives the *Jesus Seminar* some worldwide publicity.

Every generation has a few "liberal theologians". They come and go. I don't mean to put these theologians in a category with cults, in the sense that they are out to start their own communal sect, but their approach to the Bible has much in common with them. Their common principle is this:

"No one else for 2,000 years has been smart enough to really understand the New Testament. I'm the only one who can understand this very complicated piece of literature, so there's no point in reading it for yourself. You need my 'special understanding' to get the true meaning."

This "special-knowledge" claim lies behind all cults. It is the key to understanding how seemingly rational people can be led to believe and act against logic, "interpreting" quite straightforward verses of the Bible in outrageous ways. Once the cult leader (or the radical theologian!) convinces people that they alone have this "special knowledge", they are then in a position to manipulate people any way they like, because they can "interpret" the Bible to say anything they want.

Like a pulpit on a string

Whether it's cult leaders like Jim Jones and David Koresh or liberal theologians like Bishop John Spong or the *Jesus Seminar* scholars, they all keep their respective audiences hoodwinked into *not*

117

reading the New Testament for themselves, because it needs their "special interpretation". This puts them in a position where they can gain power, make lots of money with book sales, or just present themselves as superior to the rest of us. If people bothered to read the New Testament themselves, they would quickly see just how much these "interpreters" have twisted things to say what they want.

If all Jesus' teachings were meant to be parables, with the words having other meanings, then how do you explain the fact that Jesus *tells* us when he's speaking in parables and then often explains their meaning? Distinguishing his use of parables from his plain statements contradicts any idea that the Bible is *all* parables or double meanings.

The problem for these theologians and cult leaders with their different "interpretations" is that the New Testament itself claims that its letters can be "read and understood" by *anyone*, with no need for special interpretations or codes at all![102] No one is trying to say you could possibly take in the whole New Testament and understand all of it in one reading, but according to the book:

You can read it for yourself!

When you have, then you can reject it or accept it as truthful eyewitness testimony. But let's not have any "patronizing nonsense" about it being all a matter of interpretations.

The Da Vinci Code is "cracked"

At least the interpretations of Dan Brown's *The Da Vinci Code* are acknowledged fiction. Nevertheless the inference that the book is

118

based on fact doesn't square with Brown's preferred source, *The Gospel of Philip*. This "Gospel" is dated into the third century AD and that makes it even later and more spurious than the *Gospel of Thomas*. As N.T. Wright points out, "That puts it as long after Jesus' life as we are today after the time of George the Second, when Handel and Bach were writing music and George Washington was a small boy... It tells us a good deal about third-century practice in the Gnostic sect which wrote it, but nothing of any value about the first century."

Brown's idea that the council of Nicaea in AD 325 was the first time Christ was proclaimed as God, makes for a nice "conspiracy theory" for *The Da Vinci Code*, but doesn't have much relationship to real history. As we have already seen, the record of the first three centuries was replete with Jesus' claim to be God, coming not only from Christian sources, but Roman and Jewish historians. Brown's story also includes the idea that Constantine and the Nicene council "decided" on which books would be part of the Bible. The parallel with the Nicene Council in AD 325 is that they did not so much "decide" on what was in or out of the Bible, but openly declared that those texts obviously written centuries after the events with no authentic eyewitness value needed to be rejected for what they were. Only texts clearly written by those who were with Christ could be included. Thus the late fictonal Gnostic Gospels of Thomas and Philip were out. Now you might ask, if it was so obvious that they were spurious, why did they have to make it official? It seems the council's reasons for "canonising" have been vindicated by the 21st century. Here we are nearly two millennia on and people are still taking seriously fictional texts written centuries after the events of Christ while neglecting to read the accounts of those who lived with Christ.

How cults grow – more tips in cultivation

It's not practical to show you here all the documentation I've collected exposing the fraudulent activities of Bible-quoting cults, but if I did you would probably react with something like, "How could those people be fooled like that?" But they've been fooled for the same reason as sceptics who "know all about" Christianity, yet misunderstand the most basic doctrines in the New Testament. Because – they've never really read it!

The basic history surrounding the New Testament has been readily available from the first century up to this day, and it's not really a big mystery. The mystery to me is why so many people will not bother reading the New Testament themselves, but will eagerly swallow any "latest theory" that comes along, whether it ignores history or not. So many people study the critics and their books with fervour but never read the source that is being criticized.

But why? If the historical background and New Testament are relatively straightforward, why is there such eagerness for a latest theory? Why do these few "liberal" theologians gain such media coverage and public followings? (Their books sell millions, while thousands of outstanding books by Christian theologians, including many former sceptics, can be found only in Christian bookstores.) Why is the Bible eagerly "interpreted" above all other religious and secular texts? Why do people want to invent a new "history" for Jesus, while the more scant historical information on other religious leaders remains relatively uncontroversial? Where *is* the search for the real historical Buddha?

The answers to these questions belong well and truly in the previous appendix. There is a good reason why people *really want* basic Christianity not to be true. We want a piece of Jesus, but not too big a piece. We want the Jesus of love, but not the Jesus of justice. We want Jesus the great teacher, but not Jesus the God. We even want a Jesus we "believe in", but not the Lord of our life. Remember how simple the "good news" is. "If you confess Jesus as *Lord* then you will be saved." We can't ignore the Jesus of history, so we'll take any piece of him that anyone makes up, as long as we don't have to deal with the one who says he is "the Lord" and tells us to give up our guns.

The Dead Sea Scroll-duggery

We see an example of "controversial" media coverage in the reporting of the discovery of the Dead Sea Scrolls. Some media reports have attempted to imply a "Christian cover-up" by the authorities in charge of the Dead Sea Scrolls. The only thing covered up, however, is that such control by Christians is impossible. As N.T. Wright, Bishop of Durham, points out:

Most of the authorities in question are either Jewish or agnostic…it has been made clear time and time again by serious scholars from all backgrounds, Jewish, Christian and those of other religions or none, that this [cover-up] is not the case.[103]

If anyone discovered a first-century manuscript that contradicted Christian doctrine, they'd make more money than Barbara Thiering and Bishop Spong made together. But there has been no such discovery. Instead, all we have is people "interpreting" the manuscripts we do have, with "codes" that even Maxwell Smart couldn't have figured out.

If there was anything genuinely controversial in the Dead Sea Scrolls, wouldn't we have been offered something more thoughtful since 1947 than a theory that the word "all" really means "Herod Agrippa I"?

Déjà-vu Déjà-vu Déjà-vu Déjà-vu

There is one more common denominator between cults and liberal theologians that explains this "interpretations" issue. (Have we been here before?) They both begin from a position they *want* to prove, rather than seeing what the *evidence* suggests.

Claiming to be enlightened interpreters of the Bible, they – the Jehovah's Witnesses, for instance – begin with a desire to have their "piece of Jesus" and the Bible, but dislike some of the Bible's teachings, such as the deity of Christ (too hard to understand) and hell (don't want to understand!). The Jehovah's Witness leaders have made up outlandish interpretations attempting to explain away these teachings. In this way they try to make the Bible attractive to others who share their prejudices. (Unfortunately, some of the doctrines they've "made up" have caused the deaths of thousands of people, but that's another story.) See if you can spot the cult resemblance to our liberal theologians, who see themselves as anything but cult-like.

As two examples, "Barbara and the Bishop" never even tried to hide the fact that their radical Bible "interpretations" started out with a bias against some of the New Testament doctrines. With their minds already made up against certain key Bible teachings, they then went in search of a way to justify their biases. Often when Bishop Spong was interviewed he would say how he had started out with a desire to find a way to alter Christianity. His three grown daughters had rejected Christianity and he wanted to make it more "saleable" to them, because they didn't "like" it the way it was.

Similarly, the opening page of Thiering's book *Jesus the Man* carries a quote from *The Times* explaining the book's beginnings:

> [After] a deep involvement with the Church and then frustrations with certain doctrines, she became interested in the history of religion.

If these "scholars" had stumbled on some new evidence in their studies, their bias wouldn't be showing quite so much. Beginning studies of religion "*after* frustrations with certain doctrines" and "*after* not liking Christianity the way it is", is not a scholarly or objective approach. They went in search of something that was more to their liking and they twiddled those "interpretations" until they found it. This is the stuff from which religious cults are made.

After these kinds of people have twisted and contorted the New Testament out of shape (until it fits the way they "like" it), then

123

someone else who has never read it comes along and says, "See, I told you the Bible is all a matter of interpretations."

You took the words right out of my thesaurus

The liberal theologians acknowledge that there is some value in the New Testament. They say there are some truths to be found in it, but *they* must tell us which bits can be relied upon. Of course a massive ego is required to "play God", telling others which portions are the eternal truths and which ones we must throw out. But this brings me to another of your questions, "Even if Jesus was telling the truth, what if the Bible writers gave their own views as well?"

Well, if Jesus was truthful in his claim to be God, then this is an impossibility. We dealt with this earlier in noting that it was Jesus who promised guidance in the writing of the Bible, through God's own Spirit. But let's look at it further. If somehow the apostles misquoted Jesus, or sneaked in a few of their own ideas, then they must have outsmarted God (Jesus), who promised his Spirit to guide them into all truth. We would have to imagine Jesus as Lord, sitting up there in heaven, saying, "Well I gave them my words, but that darned apostle Paul was so cagey, he misquoted me and slipped in his own ideas and now I'm stuck here and I can't do anything about it." (Hey, if any of the apostles outsmarted God, maybe we should listen to them anyway!)

Remember my pyramid diagram near the end of Chapter 7? If Jesus wasn't a liar or a lunatic, then we can know for sure that the Bible is *exactly* the way God intended it to be for us.

No! – translators are not *latent dress-wearers*

"Aren't all the Bible translations different?"

There is no big deal here. The different translations in wide use today are mostly translated by teams of the best-qualified scholars from the original languages (Hebrew, Aramaic and Koine Greek), and they use the oldest available manuscripts. The translators with the best credentials often come from different faith backgrounds; some are not even Christian, which belies the idea of biased "inserts" or "deletions". If you pick up two different translations and compare them for yourself, you'll soon see that the essential difference between them is not in their meanings, but in their style and use of English. Many English words have changed in meaning dramatically since the King James Bible was translated. Many modern readers also find the older translations with their use of "thee", "thou" and "thy" somewhat awkward to read. I hope this dost showeth thee a good reason whyist there is a real need for new translations.

While there is a need to have new translations that keep up with the changes in our English language, the original languages, fortunately, are staying put. For example, the New Testament was written in Koine Greek, which is a dead language, meaning it is no longer spoken. Therefore it doesn't go through the "evolution" of, say, English, and by some strange "coincidence" it has remained unchanged over the last 2,000 years. Thanks to recent archaeological finds (such as the Dead Sea Scrolls), modern scholars actually have more knowledge of the ancient biblical languages than has been available for many centuries.

One man's meat-head is another man's parson?

So does the excuse "it's all a matter of interpretations" really stack up? If you strip away the cults and liberal theologians, both of whom use the Bible selectively, you'll find that the basic Bible doctrines have remained intact for 2,000 years. Read it yourself and you'll see its basic message could not be more straightforward:

> Either believe and follow Jesus and escape judgment, or go your own way and end up in hell.

What could be more simple? Ironically, if we were discussing any document except the New Testament, then it is the "interpretations" that would be thrown out and the New Testament would be simply taken for what it is.

Appendix (iv)

If cults are deceived, how do you know you're not?

As you know, I started out trying to be open to all possibilities. After all, how do you really know the Jehovah's Witnesses are not right if you haven't given them an open-minded investigation? I did investigate them, and other similar organizations. What I found is that it is relatively easy to obtain documentation showing that, unfortunately, leaders of cults such as Jehovah's Witnesses and Mormons deceive their followers.

Why do cult followers never get to see this material? Because such cults do not welcome critical examination. In fact, leading American cult expert Steven Hassan notes in his book *Combatting Cult Mind Control* that a common feature of cults is that they all have laws forbidding their people to look at any critical material.[104]

Bear in mind I'm not making a judgment on the average Jehovah's Witness or Mormon, because most are quite sincere people who are not deliberately deceiving anyone. However, their leaders certainly are, and some of this documentation (mostly written by the leaders themselves) is sitting on my bookshelf.

But back to your question. If people can be deceived by cults, how do I know that I'm not also deceived? If I'm open-minded it has to be possible. My immediate response is summed up in the words:

I know whom I have believed...[105]

The only one I've believed in is Jesus Christ himself. I've not "believed" in any other mediator (church or religion) who could have interpreted their version of Christ to me, because I went straight to the source. If I've been deceived it can only be by Christ himself (and you've already seen why I find untenable the idea of Jesus as a deceiver).

I can't have been deceived by the Presbyterian church I'm attending, or the Wesleyans, the Baptists, the Church of Christ or any of the others that I've attended. None of these churches could have deceived me because my beliefs neither were found in them nor relied on them. My starting point was Christ and his teachings in the New Testament. The fundamental difference between religious cult followers and the average Christian is that the cult member has their "faith" in human leaders. How do I know I'm not deceived? Because I have trusted Christ alone.

Religionnaires disease?

You asked me, "Why go to church at all, then?" Have I just caught some "religious bug"? The main reason is that I am someone who has been honest with the consequences of believing in Christ as Lord.

Church was one of the more difficult steps for me. I was still a bit prejudiced against people who went to church, and pride made it difficult to go. In addition to this, I was also playing the old "why can't I just accept him as Lord from my place?" trick.

No person or church could have changed my mind, either. I would still have that attitude now but I found that Jesus gave clear teaching relating to this matter. Firstly, he said:

If you love me, you will obey what I command.[106]

Secondly, it was *his* teaching that tells us to worship as an assembly or church.[107]

Because I had come to believe in him as Lord, I couldn't ignore going to church any more than I could "believe" that a truck was about to run me over, and not step out of the way.

Just 'cause you've gained an inch or two doesn't make you a ruler

The key distinction between Bible-centred churches and religious cults is where they locate authority. Even the most learned minister in a Bible-believing church expects his congregation to "test" him against the scriptures to see that he is teaching according to Christ's teaching in the Bible. He does not ask for blind obedience to what *he* believes or interprets. The cult leader asks us to put confidence in him. He makes himself an additional "mediator", someone coming between us – the ordinary people – and God.

We should be wary of any church that claims its own authority apart from the Bible. The reason for this is that the Bible makes it clear that there is no human religious authority on Earth, apart from Christ and his word. Christ is the only appointed head of the church.[108] In fact, the Bible goes much further. Paul the apostle says:

> *Even if we [the apostles] or an angel from heaven should preach a gospel other than the one we preached to you [New Testament], let him be eternally condemned!*

And (just in case you weren't paying attention, kids!) in the next line he says:

> *As we have already said, so now I say again: If anybody is preaching to you [another gospel]... let him be eternally condemned!*[109]

Clearly, any church that adds laws (even "good news") to the Bible, or claims to have the authority to do so, is denying the Bible itself.

Many people (even some churches) look down on those who acknowledge the Bible as their only supreme authority. But who has the more consistent approach? Logically (surely even an atheist would agree), the Bible is either true or it's not. It claims to be the written word of God. This is also either true or it's not. If it's not, then let's throw the whole lot out. There's no logic left when we set about selecting bits we "like", leaving out others, and adding a few rules of our own when the book itself clearly says "no extras".

Don't cry for me, Agitator

Part of your original question here was, "What if you're wrong anyway?" What if Jesus was a deceiver, and you're living under a delusion (along with another 2 billion or so professing Christians)? Well, the worst scenario is, I have a happy life but when I die it turns out I was wrong. Poor me.

But wait a minute. How about equal time on this business of "what if I'm wrong?" The big question is:

What if *you* are wrong?

Now things are really "hotting" up! Next appendix, please.

Appendix (v)

Why would a God of love have a hell?

You often hear people say, "I believe some things in the Bible, but I don't think a loving God would have a hell."

Again, the Bible is either true or it isn't. If it's true, it says itself that it is all true! ("All scripture is God-breathed." [110])

Over many centuries, artists (right down to today's moviemakers) have created a distorted picture of hell. Generally today, society treats as make-believe what Jesus Christ taught as a matter of sober reality. In fact, Jesus mentions hell more times than any other person or writer in the New Testament.

The umpire strikes back

The hell described in the Bible is nothing more or less than justice. It is not some collective vat where people are thrown indiscriminately. It is a place where each person meets justice, and is punished according to the degree of *their* wrongdoing, "according to what they have done" [111].

Obviously, it's still a place to be avoided at all costs. That is, if you've ever done anything wrong!

But why would a loving God have such a place?

If God is not *just*, as well as *loving*, and there is no punishment, the bad guys win! (Just try philosophically grappling with that and still calling God love.) If God does not punish evil then God is saying evil is all right. He is tolerant of evil.

Think about it. If there's no justice in the next world, where "God will bring every deed into judgment",[112] then the most malicious mass murderers and rapists come out in front. Way out in front! They are just as well off indulging in as much wrongdoing as possible. The more they get away with, the further they come out ahead of others, because they will be given more leniency. They will receive the same non-punishment as lesser wrongdoers.

...or is it? – the empire's back on strike

Those who create their own "God of the Bible with no hell" are effectively saying, "God's hands are tied and evil triumphs over God". The vilest child molester and murderer can mock God and say, "Well what's God gonna do about it?" And their answer is, "Nothing"!

The cruellest of murderers will be no worse off than their victim. That is not justice. I don't think it's love either!

Take a look at the world. There is unjust suffering and evil all over. There is no equitable answer in any philosophy or belief that doesn't include a future judgment.

There's quite a *fuhrore* in the neighbourhood

What do you say to the idea, "Let everyone go to heaven"? If that is justice and love, then I just hope I don't get a room next to an

133

unrepentant Mr Hitler, since my mother's maiden name was Cohen.

If the God of the Bible is true, on the "other side" justice will be met, and "every deed judged". Only a perfect, loving, just God, who knows the hearts and minds of all people, would be in a position to administer that justice fairly.

It's a hell of a motivation

"It can't be right if God is motivating us by a fear of hell," you say. But if the reason for the fear is a fact, it doesn't necessarily follow that this is just a way for God to motivate us.

Hell is a necessary consequence of a person's moral choice to do wrong and is the means of dealing justly with it. Hell is not a cruel creation of God to motivate people by fear. It is the response of a just God to all that is wrong.

If we have never done anything wrong then there is no need to fear punishment. It is because of *our* actions that we need to fear hell.

It would even be logical and fair for a perfectly just God to intend punishing our wrongs, without ever warning us. In which case we would have no fear until it was too late. Thankfully, God is loving as well as just. A God who is just not only doesn't have to warn us, he certainly doesn't have to provide an escape clause for us either. Only a God of love would do that.

It's also important not to confuse fear of punishment with the godly fear referred to in the Bible. Godly fear is a true reverence and awe for God that even Jesus had for his Father (Hebrews 5:7).

134

But in relation to punishment, the Bible assures us that "perfect love drives out fear" (1 John 4:18). There can be no fear of punishment for those who have Jesus as their Lord and substitute, because Jesus has already been punished in their place at the cross. You can't be punished twice for the same crime.

Soul-diers of fortune

So is hell a scare tactic to recruit religious followers? There have always been those who will exploit "the fear of God" as a way of gaining money or power in the name of religion. So what! There are also plenty of us who use these "scaremongers" as a cop-out to reject open-minded investigation of religion.

Our big excuse for not checking things out is that the world is full of religions and churches that are fakes trying to scare people into following them. Therefore, all organized religions and churches are fake. This is a ridiculous generalization. Obviously there are fakes, but remember there are two things that are essential to counterfeiting:

1. There is always an original that is copied.
2. The original is always of value (no one counterfeits Monopoly money).

Once again I would ask you not to assess things on the basis of "people" who have abused the "fear of God" for their own gain, but to read the source. Go for the original!

The hell-sinky is overflowing

There's a "hell" in all the major religions. All the major religions have this reason for "fear". They all have the concept that all our wrongdoing must be accounted and paid for. It seems that almost universally the conscience of man says there is right and wrong and punishment.

For example, the Buddhist description of hell and punishment for sin is so graphic it makes Freddy Krueger look like just another kid with acne. Here's a small sample:

> [The person in hell is]…trimmed with hatchets…needle-mouthed creatures successively rip away his skin, hide, flesh, sinews…so they can munch his marrow…they prize open his mouth with a red-hot iron crowbar, and push into his mouth a red-hot ball of copper…that passes out below taking with it the bowels and intestines.[113]

Hell is a fundamental doctrine of Buddhist teaching, and yet you don't generally hear a lot about it. Perhaps they believe they will reach more people if they don't mention it? But if a religion is true and there really is a hell, then wouldn't you want to know about it? And wouldn't it be more loving to be warned?

Fear is a state of mind –
no fear is a state of *no* mind

Throughout our lives we see the connection between love and warning through fear. Like God in the Bible, if we love someone we warn them of danger. Look at the way we use fear to warn our children of the danger of fire, of crossing the road or of talking to strangers. It seems in all our lives we are safeguarded by *fears*. All for our own good.

Only a fool has "no fear" when crossing a busy street, but that doesn't make cars a bad thing.

If Christ was telling the truth, then he is God. That is quite simple. Because he is loving, he warned us in advance of the need for justice – and that hell was a reality.

But to us it's reality, shmality. In childhood and adulthood, our pride says we just don't like being told for our good what we should fear – and it's often to our detriment.

The hell truth and nothing but...

If the New Testament is true then hell cannot be a place of cruelty. If hell was cruel, then how could heaven be heaven? The New Testament tells us heaven is a place of great joy where there is no more sorrow, no pain or tears, and yet there will be an awareness that there are those in hell.[114]

How could anyone be without sorrow in heaven, knowing others are being punished, *unless they were satisfied that it was completely fair and just?* (Perhaps this thought also gives a glimpse

137

of how much those in heaven would be aware that they had escaped that which *they also* truly deserved.)

I don't think we can ever really deal with the concept of hell until we can accept that God's holy justice, so far beyond our comprehension, is a right and good thing; that God is righteous, and we aren't. And yet we do comprehend the idea of justice for wrongdoing. We don't expect criminals to be set free because they are sorry. We think jail is a good thing (for them). *Not a good place to be* but a good thing to have. Even the most hardened inmate thinks jail is a good thing, even if he thinks *he* "doesn't belong there". Even in our imperfect way, by admitting jail is a good thing to have, we are acknowledging hell is also a good thing.

You're carrying a big load on your shoulders (apart from your dandruff)

If you make up your own "god", one without a hell, you have to realize this "god" is in total opposition to the God of the Bible. And you guessed it: Jesus must have been lying about hell too!

Rita, don't be too quick to laugh at cults like the Jehovah's Witnesses. A God with no hell is one of their main things. It's one of the big carrots they dangle to prospective followers, and here you are, falling for it too.

"I'll believe in my own 'God' because he doesn't have a nasty old hell; he's a loving God."

This reminds me of the Jews mentioned in the Old Testament who turned from God and carved their own gods. We say, "How could they be so silly as to believe in a god they made themselves, one the Bible says they could 'carry on their own shoulders' "[115]? But if you have a God with no justice or hell, you too are carrying around your own created god on your shoulders – inside your head! And you too are mocking the second commandment, which condemns creating your own image of God.

Appendix (vi)

Women

The next point I'll discuss is one that I found difficult to understand when I first read the Bible. I was against prejudice in any form and I found it difficult to see how equality of human beings was consistent with "wives submit to your husbands". That is, until I looked at the whole text.

Immediately after the scripture "wives submit…" we find that husbands should "love their wives, just as Christ loved the church and gave himself up for her…". A husband being the head of the family doesn't sit well with many people. But if the whole thing is taken seriously, and a husband's love for his wife is to the point of his own death, then how many wives would feel they were the loser?

God has given men and women different roles. Some have used this to suggest women have no importance in the church, but this is clearly not the case. The early church contained "prophetesses",[116] and the apostle Paul commends the great work done by females such as Phoebe.[117]

Are we willing to admit that God could have a perspective of equality beyond our comprehension? If our perspective was anything to go by, then obviously women were not created "equal" in roles anyway. Women carry and give birth to babies. This is discrimination! But how many women claim to be "inferior" because they have to go through the burden of childbearing and -birth? Obviously God gave different roles to men and women in more ways than one.

Do different roles mean that men and women are unequal? No. In terms of importance and equality before God, the New Testament makes it clear that with God:

> *... there is neither male nor female.*[118]

and:

> *In the Lord ... woman is not independent of man, nor is man independent of woman. For as woman came from man, so also man is born of woman, but everything comes from God.*[119]

Erasing all the differences between men and women doesn't make them equal, it makes them identical!

Religious *male*practice

For a moment, let's play supermarket religion and choose one we "like" on the subject of women. Let's look at the alternatives from the other major religions:

Judaism – One of the reasons Jesus got into so much trouble with the Jewish Pharisees was their man-made traditions. This included women being rejected as credible witnesses in a court of law and yet Jesus made sure it was women, in particular, who would be the first "witnesses" of his resurrection. Jesus also broke ground for

Jews at that time when he spoke to the woman at the well: not only was she not Jewish, but the disciples "were surprised to find him talking with a woman".[120]

Hinduism – Quite simply, there is no salvation for women. The only hope for woman is to be reincarnated in the next life as a man.

Islam – The Koran doesn't mince words. If you think I'm taking things out of context, please check the Koran yourself where it says men are "superior", and, if your wives are disobedient:

> …send them to beds apart and beat them.[121]

Buddhism – Buddhism has similar reincarnation beliefs to Hinduism concerning women. For anyone who is enlightened:

> …he is always a male, and never a woman.[122]

The *Lion Handbook* on *The World's Religions* makes the point that the original Buddha, Siddhartha Gautama:

> …felt women were dangerous because they kept the cycle of rebirth in motion and thus embodied the greed for life. He maintained that if women had not been admitted, his teachings would have lasted 1,000 years but now they would only last 500 years.[123]

He was about 2,000 years out with that little prophecy.

Appendix (vii)

What about those who haven't heard?

"What about those in isolated places, or babies who died in infancy, or those billions of people in China and Africa?" We say, "If they couldn't have heard of Jesus then it can't be true."

Isn't it ironic that two of the most common complaints about Christianity are, "Why do those missionaries have to go bothering those other cultures and pushing their religion?" And yet in the same breath, "What about those cultures who have never heard?" And further irony is the fact that there never have been "billions" of people who have never heard about Jesus. The world population didn't even reach 1 billion until the 20th century. Before the new millennium the population skyrocketed to over 6 billion. Coinciding with that population explosion was a worldwide communication explosion – including an explosion of the going forth of the message of Jesus. Because we think the world revolves around us in the West, we think Christianity is dying. And it is! At least, it's dying to those in the West who are rejecting their opportunity. But for a long time now Christianity has undergone massive expansion in China (growing towards 100 million Christians), along with Africa and South America, to the point that Christianity is no longer a Western world religion.

The important thing to note on this subject is that God is not caught out "over-penalizing" anyone. Remember that judgment is on an individual basis, "according to the things they have done". Jesus made it clear that the opportunity the individual has to hear about him will be one of the chief criteria used to determine his or her judgment:

> **The servant who did not know the plan…will be let off lightly.**

But Jesus brings the question back to those who have heard, saying:

> **…the servant who knows his master's will and does not get ready or act upon it…much more will be asked.**[124]

This doesn't give anyone an escape clause. The Bible tells us that each person has some knowledge of right and wrong written on their hearts. Every human being has a conscience that will work for or against them depending on how they have responded to it.[125] But the finger is pointed more squarely at those who did have the opportunity to hear. Rather than finding a loophole with this issue, those of us who have had the opportunity to hear of Jesus condemn ourselves when using "the lack of opportunity of others" as an excuse. The New Testament speaks to those of us in "civilized" comfort (with the gospel) saying:

> **It would have been better for them not to have known the way of righteousness, than to have known it and then to turn [away].**[126]

144

A tale of two-timing cities

Jesus actually went as far as to say that the two most notorious "sin cities" of the ancient world, Sodom and Gomorrah, would not come under as harsh a judgment as those people who simply reject their own opportunity to believe in Jesus.[127] Every time someone points at some "remote tribe" as a reason for not responding to God, I can't help but think that those pointing the finger are in much bigger trouble.

What about those who haven't heard? I'm much more worried about many of those who *have*!

Appendix (viii)

Why does God allow suffering?

I had this question for some time, too. After studying the holy books of all the religions, I found there is a good answer in the Bible.

There is no explanation in philosophy or atheism. In fact, the atheist who asks, "Why suffering?" is left with an even worse problem. If there is no God, how is suffering and evil even wrong? After all, who determines what is right and wrong?

If it's left to individual opinion then the murderer and child molester who don't think they've done wrong, or even those who have no compassion for starving Africans "because it balances out our resources", are just as "right" as anyone. Unless there is an absolute, all "wrongs", even those that actually hurt someone else, become subjective. Without an absolute authority there are no rights and wrongs, only opinions.

Can opinions ever establish moral ethics?

If you think so, then you haven't thought through the implications of our individuality. No two persons are alike or can agree 100% on right and wrong. I even spoke to a young guy in prison who murdered someone, and he thought murder was "fair enough, if the person really deserved it". And, you know something, if there's no God who says "You shall not murder", who is to say that that young man doesn't have an argument?

"Oh, but most people know right from wrong."

Certainly! As long as it's *your* opinion as to who the "most" are, and *your* opinion as to what is "right" and "wrong".

No two opinions will ever agree on who exactly the "most" are. People are often evenly divided over contentious moral issues, rather than a majority versus a minority. Anyone who says *they* can determine where the lines are drawn in ethics, is playing God. (Is that irony? There are atheists out there like Professor Peter Singer who are playing God!)

Karma back again

Buddhism and Hinduism say suffering comes from the individual's karma. The result is reincarnation. The starving child or the woman who is raped "brought it on themselves; it was their karma", their payback for the kind of person they are in this life, or for the person they were in a previous life, which they now have no control over. Either way, the molested child or murder victim "deserved it". Are millions of starving children getting the "just deserts" of their reincarnation?

It is fashionable for Westerners to make up their own idea of reincarnation. Many have done this, including Shirley MacLaine. The result is that everyone gets to be an Egyptian prince or princess in a previous life. But let's deal with what the originators of reincarnation say. Westerners who "make up" their own version of reincarnation are effectively saying the Hindus and Buddhists don't know what they're talking about.

147

Life – it's a dead end

In contrast, Jesus made it clear several times that an individual's suffering in this life is not necessarily a result of their own bad deeds.[128] In fact the New Testament is totally opposed to reincarnation:

> **Man is destined to die once, and after that to face judgment.**[129]

Rather than being created robots or living at the mercy of our previous lives, the Bible says that we are each born as a genuinely new life, with an individual will and responsibility. Cause and effect is natural to both science and God. When man became corrupted – God responded appropriately. The effect was that corruption entered the world and ruined all that was originally good, even the natural world itself. (Remember my analogy with the cyanide in the glass of milk? One drop corrupts the lot!)

All kinds of natural chaos and suffering have resulted as a flow-on effect of man's corruption and his rejection of God. Because of this, the Bible says, "the whole creation has been groaning" and is in "bondage to decay".[130] (It's worth noting that science has observed this process of breakdown and decay and describes its operation in the natural world in the second law of thermodynamics as "entropy".) This was not God's "arbitrary decision", but an inevitable consequence of man's rejection of all that was good. A necessary cause/effect judgment on man's corruption.

Are you without fault?
The first time ever eye-sore your face

But, hey, you and I are not personally responsible for corruption coming into the world. Are we? Well, Rita, if we could remove everyone in history who ever did wrong, and just leave you and your choice of friends, would wrongdoing ever get a fresh start? Of course. We have to share the responsibility. We are not just victims but part of the problem; we are not just collectively guilty, but individually guilty as well.

Lord, change me! – but not yet (St Augustine)

Much of the world's suffering is a matter of man's inhumanity to man. This is a second aspect of the same problem. But are you still open to an explanation of suffering if we can't blame God?

In our society we demand our individual freedom. The last bastions of communism are falling. Individual choice and freedom are more than just a dream: they are celebrated as a reality and as a right. What do we do with our freedom?

People make choices that cause pain and suffering. They do this directly through crime, preying upon other people. They do this indirectly, too, or by what they fail to do. For instance, we neglect the needs of the starving while there is enough food on this planet for everyone.

And we blame *God* for this?

We all scream for our own rights and responsibility. Well, *we've got them!* But, like the genie who grants the three wishes, you have

149

got to live with the consequences and you can't blame the giver of the gift for the consequences if things go wrong. (It needs to be said that, according to the Bible, God has a plan for cleaning up the whole mess anyway, and we're getting to that.) But we want to have our cake and eat it. We ask, "Well, why did he make us this way?" (Like we know more than God!) And yet how many of us want to give up our "right" to have our own moral choices and would prefer to be a robotic clone, mechanically forced to make certain moral choices and obey God?

Why doesn't God stop the bad guys now?

Man's wrong moral choices are a chief cause of suffering in the world. The only real question left is, "Why doesn't God stop evil behaviour right now?"

Of course, God could eliminate our moral choice and wipe out evil now. That's no problem for God, but it's a big problem for us! A perfect God might well decide to administer complete and perfect justice immediately, but then he would have to eliminate *all* evil, not just the "really bad guys". There can be no half measures with *perfect* justice.

What if God decided to get rid of everyone who did anything wrong between now and lunchtime tomorrow? By afternoon tea the cafeteria would be empty! Instead, life goes on and we are still here. Why? The New Testament says why:

The Lord is not slow in keeping his promise [to bring judgment to the whole world], as some understand slowness. He is patient

150

***with you, not wanting anyone to perish, but everyone to come
to repentance.***[131]

Instead of asking why God doesn't intervene and stop evil now, we
should be jumping for joy that he *hasn't*. Despite his promise of
eventual complete judgment, he has waited patiently for those who
will repent and receive his forgiveness before he judges "every
deed". He has waited for you and me.

Watch out for hardening of the hearteries

It's a cop-out to blame God for not preventing man's wrong
choices, when the only choices we want stopped are the "other
guys'", not ours.

I look back and remember that, like you, I asked the question,
"Why is there suffering and evil in the world if there is a loving
God?" It's ironic that some think that suffering and evil are a
stumbling block for Christianity to explain, when in fact suffering
and evil are half of the very explanation of Christianity itself!
That is, man, given his own choice, corrupts a good gift.
Thankfully, that is only half the explanation of Christianity. There
is also good news. According to the God of the Bible, there is a
master plan for restoration in the afterlife.

No matter how much injustice there is in this life, all will be set
right at judgment, when "every deed *good and bad*, including every
hidden thing, will be judged".

Not only will everyone who inflicts suffering be punished

151

appropriately, but those who have suffered righteously will be "richly rewarded" in the next life.[132]

I'm not suggesting that this removes the pain we feel now when we see the reality of evil and suffering about us. But it does mean a great deal to know that God is going to bring justice and an end to the world's evil and suffering.

The God of the Bible promises a better life ahead: "life to the full", joyful and full of things that are "inexpressible",[133] "no more death or mourning or crying or pain",[134] no more suffering and evil. Until then, he has told us all we need to know:

> *Now we see but a poor reflection; then we shall see face to face. Now I know in part; then I shall know fully, even as I am fully known.*[135]

Notes

1. Repentance 9:73, The Koran
2. Woman 4:86–91, The Koran
3. R. Humphries and R. Ward, *Religious Bodies in Australia* (Melbourne, 1988) p.XI
4. Interviewer Sam Newman, *Herald-Sun* Melbourne 17.6.92 pp.34–35
5. R.C. Sproul, *Nothing Left to Chance* Video Series (Florida: Ligonier)
6. Meditation, *Buddhist Scriptures* (England: Penguin, 1959) p.113
7. Ibid., pp.76, 77
8. Repentance 9:30, The Koran
9. The Table 5:70–73, The Koran
10. John 5:18
11. C.C. Ryrie, *Basic Theology* (Victor Books, 1986) p.248
12. 1 Kings 20:35
13. John 10:30–33
14. John 20:28
15. John 20:28–29
16. Pliny, *Epistles* 10:96
17. Cited from Jewish historian Joseph Klausner, *Jesus of Nazareth*, translated from the original Hebrew by Danby (London: The Macmillan Co., 1925) pp.34–35
18. C.S. Lewis, *Mere Christianity* (London: Collins Fountain Paperbacks, 1952) p.52
19. J.T. Fisher MD and Lowell S. Hawley, *A Few Buttons Missing: A Case Book of a Psychiatrist* (Lippincott, 1951) p.273
20. R. Morey, *The New Atheism* (Bethany House Publishers, 1986) p.134

21. Josephus, *Antiquities of the Jews*, 18:3:63–64
22. *Annals of Imperial Rome*, Tacitus 15:44, 2–5
23. Mark 14:61–62
24. John 19:34
25. *Annals of Imperial Rome*, Tacitus 15:44, 2–5
26. Acts 1:21–22
27. 2 Peter 1:16
28. Matthew 26:74
29. J. McDowell, *More Than a Carpenter* (Eastbourne, Great Britain: Kingsway Publishers Ltd., 1979) p.61
30. John 7:3–5
31. Josephus, *Antiquities*, 20:197–203
32. S. Gaukroger, *It Makes Sense* (Scripture Union) p.61
33. J. McDowell, *The Resurrection* (England: Scripture Press, 1988) p.18
34. Ibid., p.101
35. Quoted from D. James Kennedy, *Evangelism Explosion* 1983 pp.102–03
36. D. Stewart, *The Ten Wonders of the Bible* (Dart Press, 1990) p.44
37. C.V. Taylor, *Bible with Holes?* (Queensland, Australia: Assembly Kingswood Publishers, 1988) p.31
38. J. McDowell, *Evidence That Demands a Verdict* (England: Here's Life Publishers, 1972) pp.40–43
39. F.F. Bruce, *The New Testament Documents* (InterVarsity Press, 1988) pp.16–17
40. F. Kenyon, *The Bible and Modern Scholarship* (London: John Murray, 1948) p.20
41. H. Morris, *Many Infallible Proofs* (Master Books, 1974) p.22
42. Stewart p.51
43. *60 Minutes* Australia, aired 22/11/92 Producer John Little, Reporter Jeff McMullin

44. Referred to in Stewart p.58
45. Kennedy pp.88–89
46. J. Fisher and P. Cummins, *Predictions* (London: Sidgwick and Jackson, 1980) pp.16–17
47. Acts 2:41; Acts 4:4
48. Matthew 28:19
49. Genesis 12:1–3
50. Matthew 28:19
51. Matthew 16:17
52. Ezekiel 11:16–17
53. Morris pp.241–42
54. Isaiah 40:22 was written circa 750 BC
55. W.E. Jackel, The Bible, p.93
56. The Overwhelming Event 88:17–20, The Koran
57. (ed.) F. Max Muller, *Buddhist Mahayana Texts Part 1 The Buddha-Karita of Asvaghosha* (Delhi: Motilal Banarsidass Publishers, 1990) p.17
58. Job 26:7
59. Job 38:16
60. S.I. McMillen, *None Of These Diseases* (London: Marshall Pickering, 1990) pp.24–25
61. Matthew 16:15
62. 2 Timothy 4:5
63. E. de Bono, *I am Right, You are Wrong* (London: Penguin Books, 1991) p.196
64. I owe this concept to J. McDowell and B. Hostetler, *Don't Check Your Brains at the Door* (Dallas: Word Publishing, 1992) pp.116–18
65. John 10:35
66. John 16:13
67. John 14:26

68. Romans 1:20
69. Luke 16:19–31
70. Ecclesiastes 12:14
71. 1 John 1:8
72. Luke 18:9–14
73. James 2:10
74. Ecclesiastes 12:14
75. 1 John 1:5
76. Hebrews 12:29
77. Romans 6:23 and Revelation 20:12
78. Matthew 27:46
79. Philippians 2:5–8
80. John 5:24, NRSV
81. Romans 5:10
82. Romans 5:7–8
83. Ephesians 2:8–9
84. Revelation 21:27
85. Romans 10:9
86. Matthew 4:17
87. Matthew 7:22–23
88. 1 John 2:4
89. (ed.) F.M. Muller, translated by various oriental scholars, *Sacred Books of the East, Dhammapada* (Delhi: Motilal Banarsidass Publishers, 1992) p.165
90. Matthew 5:3
91. W.E. Vine, Ed. F.F. Bruce, *Vine's Expository Dictionary of Old and New Testament Words* (Iowa: World Bible Publishers, 1981) p.84
92. *Christian Info News* statistics show the percentage of 33.7% has remained steady in the last 20 years
93. James 2:19

94. John 12:42–43
95. John 20:29
96. 1 Thessalonians 5:21
97. Colossians 2:8
98. 2 Timothy 4:3–5
99. 1 Peter 3:15
100. Matthew 22:36–39
101. Declared ex cathedra by Pope Pius X11 in 1950
102. 2 Corinthians 1:13
103. N.T. Wright, *Who Was Jesus?* (SPCK, 1992) pp.19, 20
104. S. Hassan, *Combatting Cult Mind Control* (Rochester, Vermont: Park Street Press, 1988) p.65
105. 2 Timothy 1:12
106. John 14:15
107. Hebrews 10:25
108. Ephesians 1:22
109. Galatians 1:8–9
110. 2 Timothy 3:16
111. Revelation 20:12
112. Ecclesiastes 12:14
113. "Torments of the Hells", *Buddhist Scriptures*, pp. 225–26
114. Revelation 21:4; Luke 16:19–31; Isaiah 66:22–24
115. Isaiah 46:7
116. Luke 2:36
117. Romans 16:1–2
118. Galatians 3:28
119. 1 Corinthians 11:11–12
120. John 4:27
121. Women 4:34, The Koran
122. *Buddhist Scriptures*, p.30

123. *A Lion Handbook, The World's Religions* (Lion Publishing, 1993) p.225
124. Luke 12:47–48
125. Romans 2:14–15
126. 2 Peter 2:21
127. Matthew 10:14–15
128. Luke 13:1–5; John 9:1–3
129. Hebrews 9:27
130. Romans 8:21–22
131. 2 Peter 3:9
132. Hebrews 10:33–35
133. 2 Corinthians 12:4
134. Revelation 21:4
135. 1 Corinthians 13:12